How to build your own PC

Other Computer Tiles

by

R. A. Penfold

BP450   How to Expand and Upgrade Your PC
BP467   How to Interface PCs
BP470   Linux for Windows users

How to build your own PC

R. A. Penfold

Bernard Babani (publishing) Ltd
The Grampians
Shepherds Bush Road
London W6 7NF
England

www.babanibooks.com

Please note

Although every care has been taken with the production of this book to ensure that any projects, designs, modifications, and/or programs, etc., contained herewith, operate in a correct and safe manner and also that any components specified are normally available in Great Britain, the Publisher and Author do not accept responsibility in any way for the failure (including fault in design) of any projects, design, modification, or program to work correctly or to cause damage to any equipment that it may be connected to or used in conjunction with, or in respect of any other damage or injury that may be caused, nor do the Publishers accept responsibility in any way for the failure to obtain specified components.

Notice is also given that if any equipment that is still under warranty is modified in any way or used or connected with home-built equipment then that warranty may be void.

© 1999 BERNARD BABANI (publishing) LTD

First Published - November 1999
Reprinted - June 2000
Reprinted - December 2000
Reprinted - March 2001
Reprinted - September 2001

British Library Cataloguing in Publication Data

A catalogue record for this book is available from the British Library

ISBN   0 85934 4797

Cover Design by Gregor Arthur
Printed and bound in Great Britain by Cox & Wyman Ltd, Reading

Preface

Although assembling a PC might seem to be something that is only suitable for experts, it is really much easier than most people realise. All the parts required are available from computer shops, mail order warehouses, and computer fairs. Whether you wish to build the most budget of budget PCs, an up-market PC using the latest high-tech components, or anything in between, all the parts required are readily available. Although one might reasonably expect building a PC to be extremely difficult, it does not require any special skills. In fact the assembly job is pretty straightforward, and it is just a matter of bolting things in place and plugging in a few cables. A crosshead screwdriver might be the only tool required, and it is unlikely that anything else apart from a pair of pliers will be needed. No soldering iron is required, and neither is any experience of electronics construction methods.

All this does not mean that PC building can be undertaken by absolutely anyone. Some experience of using and dealing with PCs is essential, and you need to be reasonably practical. Obviously some technical knowledge is needed in order to buy the right components and get everything put together properly. This book explains in simple terms exactly what components are required and how to assemble them to produce a working PC. Having built your first PC it then requires more technical knowledge to get everything set up correctly and the operating system installed. Again, this book explains in simple terms, how to get the BIOS set up correctly, and how to install popular operating systems such as Windows 98, Windows NT4, and Linux. The finished PC is unlikely to give any problems, but the final chapter deals with simple troubleshooting techniques. Using these techniques any fault should be rapidly located and rectified.

Many prospective builders worry about how well (or otherwise) a home constructed PC will perform. Whether a PC is home produced or ready made it is built using much the same components, and the level of performance should be much the same either way. The costs involved can also be a worry. With wise buying a home constructed PC will probably cost somewhat less than a ready built PC of similar specification, although any savings are not likely to be large. However, by "rolling your own" it is possible to produce a computer that exactly meets your requirements, and you will learn a great deal in the process. It is also good fun and should impress your friends!

R. A. Penfold

WARNING

Sensible safety precautions should always be observed when dealing with electrical and electronic equipment, particularly any equipment that connects to the mains supply or operates at high voltages. **Do not open the case of a monitor or a PC power supply unit.** *Apart from the fact that both of these are mains powered, they operate using high voltages that can remain on the circuit boards even after the equipment has been switched off for some time. If you use a PC connected to the mains supply as an earth for anti-static purposes, make sure that the power is switched off at the mains outlet so that the PC can not be accidentally switched on. With an AT case and power supply, examine the connections to the on/off switch before connecting the unit to the mains supply. All four connections should be completely covered by plastic insulators.* **Do not use the unit if there are any signs at all of problems with the insulation.** *Never work on a PC while it is switched on.*

Contents

3

Assembly 57

4

The BIOS 99

5

Operating systems 121

6

Troubleshooting 149

Trademarks

Fundamentals

What's involved?

Constructing your own PC may seem a daunting prospect, but it is actually much easier than most people realise. It has to be emphasised that we are not talking here in terms of getting out a soldering iron and making your own motherboard, video card, etc., or even in terms of doing some metalwork to produce your own case. Due to the predominance of specialist electronic components in the PC world, most of which are not generally available, this approach is probably not viable even for those prepared to put in the massive time and effort involved. Also, by the time your completely home-made PC was finished it would probably be well and truly out of date!

What we are really talking about here is a home assembled PC based on a set of ready-made boards and housed in a commercially produced case. Everything you need to make a PC is readily available, and the tools needed to assemble one are minimal. In fact one medium size cross-point screwdriver is quite possibly the only tool you will require. Depending on your opinion of these things, building your own PC is as easy or as difficult as putting together your own self-assembly furniture. Inevitably there are some questions that anyone contemplating PC assembly will need answered. We will consider some of the more common questions before taking a look at the basic steps involved in making your own PC. Subsequent chapters consider each of these steps in detail.

The real thing?

Having put together your PC will it work as well as the ready-made "real thing", or will you end up with a low specification PC that is incapable of running high-end software? Provided you compare like with like there is no reason for any difference in performance and capabilities between a ready-made PC and a home-made machine. It pays to bear in mind that most PC manufacturers do not actually make their own motherboards, sound cards, etc., but instead put together PCs from "off the shelf" components. In other words, most ready-made PCs are put together in the same way as a home-made PC, and apart from the nameplate a ready-made PC is no different to a home produced equivalent. Of course, if you put together a PC from all the cheapest parts you can lay your hands on it would be naive to expect it to equal the latest thing in commercially produced PC technology. With PCs, as with most things in life, you tend to get what you pay for.

Will it work?

Whether you buy a PC ready-made or make it yourself it is impossible to guarantee that it will work first time and that it will continue to work flawlessly for many years. Neither is it possible to guarantee that there will not be the odd incompatibility problem with a certain piece of hardware refusing to peacefully coexist with a certain piece of software. Provided the PC is built using good quality components and you are not tempted to cut corners it should work first time. Once it is "up and running", with average luck it should be at least a few years before a major breakdown occurs. Obviously some constructors will have worse than average luck, and will have to deal with a fault or faults. Others will fair better than average, and will not have to fix any faults during the working life of the PC, even if it is used for many years.

Home-made and ready-made PCs should both be covered by manufacturers warranties, but these operate in very different ways with the two types of PC. With a ready-made PC the manufacturers guarantee should cover the PC as a whole. If anything goes wrong the manufacturer should locate the fault and fix it for you. There may be a return to base warranty, or some form of on-site maintenance agreement. The latter is clearly preferable to the former, but is likely to be reflected in a higher price tag for the PC. In either case, unless you buy a lemon the time taken getting things put right should be reasonably short, and no technical skills will be required on your part.

With a home assembled PC you should have individual guarantees for every component in the system, but there is no manufacturer to provide an overall guarantee for the complete PC. If something goes wrong it is up to you to find out just what has gone awry and get the faulty component exchanged under warranty. Locating the faulty component is not usually too difficult, but getting it replaced quickly is not always possible. If the faulty component was ordered by mail order you will have to send it back, it is likely that it will then go through some sort of testing, and then the replacement will be sent. This could leave the PC out of action for several days. Of course, if you buy a ready-made PC by mail order and it has a return to base warranty, you have the same problem. In fact matters are worse because the whole PC often has to be returned, not just the faulty component.

This lack of speed in getting things fixed may or may not matter. Where it is important to get a PC working straight away, and to keep it working, a ready-made PC with an on-site maintenance agreement with a reputable company is the safest option. You have no absolute guarantee of quick fixes, but there is a good chance of keeping any downtimes to a minimum. You may find a company prepared to offer on-site maintenance on a home constructed PC, but this is by no means certain.

The odd incompatibility problem is likely to be difficult to solve whether you buy a ready-made PC or build one yourself. Whoever you complain to, it is always the other company's fault! Fortunately, this type of thing is much more rare than it was, and it is probably not a major issue any more.

Will I save money?

Many people try their hand at DIY PC construction in an attempt to save money. Provided you purchase the individual components wisely it is likely that there will be a small cost saving. However, do not expect to get a half price PC by building it yourself. A saving of around 10 percent is certainly quite possible, and with careful buying you may even achieve a saving of as much as 20 percent or so. On the other hand, with imprudent buying you could easily end up paying 10 or 20 percent more for your PC. Assembling a PC takes no more than a very few hours work, and it would be unrealistic to expect the DIY approach to produce massive cost savings.

It is probably not the assembly costs that account for the majority of the savings anyway. When you buy a new PC it generally comes complete with some form of support package such as a one-year onsite maintenance contract and some sort of telephone support system. With a home produced PC you have to be more self-sufficient. There may well be telephone or Email support for some of the components, but in general it is up to you to sort things out when problems arise. If you are able to sort out these problems yourself it makes sense to do so rather than pay for support that you do not really need, and will probably never use.

Can I do it?

As pointed out previously, actually putting the computer together does not require a great deal of skill. Someone who is completely impractical would be well advised not to attempt building a PC, or anything else for that matter. Provided you are not a DIY disaster waiting to happen, you should be able to physically put the PC together. This is not to say that anyone who can use a screwdriver is properly qualified to build a PC. When dealing with computers odd little problems tend to develop, particularly when dealing with device drivers and software installation. Someone with a few years experience of using PCs should be able to sort out these problems without too much difficulty. For "old hands" at computing this sort of thing is just part of the fun. For a newcomer to PCs it could be difficult and time consuming to get the finished product set up and really working well. In fact it could be difficult to get the PC set up and working at all. Consequently, I would only recommend PC assembly if you have had a few years experience with PCs and are not going to panic if minor problems occur.

Why bother?

If constructing your own PC is not going to save large amounts of money, and you will have to sort out any minor problems yourself, why bother? Although any savings in cost are not likely to be huge, a worthwhile saving can still be made. Alternatively, for the same money it should be possible to produce a PC with a higher specification by doing it yourself. Also, many people find that making their own PC is a fun and interesting experience. If you like making things, having built one PC it is unlikely that you will return to the world of ready-made PCs. I suppose that for many people the kudos of building your own PC is another plus point. It is a good way to impress your friends.

For most PC builders the main advantage is that you can build a PC having the exact specification you require. Many PC companies will to some extent customise one of their standard PCs to suit your requirements, but few will build one to your exact specification. By doing it yourself you can have the video and soundcards you deem the best, the most suitable monitor for your requirements, and so on. If you only need a small hard disc drive but need an advanced 3D-video card and large monitor, then that is what you buy. The time you save in searching for a PC with the right specification at the right price should be more than enough to build the PC yourself. Financial constraints may force a few compromises, but you should end up with the best possible PC for your requirements, or something as near to it as the available money permits.

Another potential advantage of building your own is that it may be possible to use parts from your previous PC. Being realistic about it, there will probably be few (if any) original parts from an old PC that will be suitable for a new one. A few items such as the mouse, keyboard, and floppy disc drive will probably be usable if they are in good condition, but little else is likely to be of much use. However, most PCs get a certain amount of upgrading over the years, and any recent additions to the old PC will probably be useable in the new one. For example, a recently added CD-ROM drive, sound card, or loudspeaker system is usually suitable for transplanting into a new PC. Again, the saving in cost is not likely to be huge, but the cost of the new PC can be significantly reduced without severely compromising its performance.

One final point that is worth making is that you will learn a great deal about PCs by building your own. Constructing a PC will not turn you into a computer expert overnight, but you will certainly learn a great deal about the way everything functions. If any problems arise in the future or you wish to upgrade a PC it should be much easier to sort things out once you have some experience of PC construction.

Getting started

Having decided to "take the plunge" and build your own PC the first task is to make a list of all the components required, complete with brief notes detailing any special requirements. You may already have a fair idea of what you require, but otherwise it is a matter of studying reviews in computer magazines and looking through magazine advertisements in order to find the best components at a price you can afford. If your aim is merely to produce a PC at a "rock bottom" price it becomes more matter of scanning the advertisements for "special offers" and touring the local computer fairs for the best deals you can obtain. Before buying any "bargain" components make sure that they are compatible with the other items in the system, and are not totally out of date. Be particularly wary of very cheap motherboards, as these often require obsolete processors and memory modules that cost a great deal and give relatively poor performance. If components are offered at very low prices there is usually a catch somewhere.

1 Fundamentals

This list represents the minimum you will require in order to produce a working PC.

Case with PSU, set of fixing screws, etc

Motherboard with cables, etc

Memory modules to suit the motherboard

Microprocessor with matching heatsink and fan

Keyboard and mouse

Video card

Monitor

3.5 inch floppy disc drive

Hard disc drive

CD-ROM drive

A CD-ROM drive used to be considered something of a luxury, but as most software is now supplied on CD-ROMs you will probably not get far without one. For multimedia applications, voice recognition, etc., you will also require a sound card and speakers plus (possibly) a headset and microphone. You may also require other items such as a printer and a modem, but here we will only consider the main constituent parts of the PC itself. It is advisable to put together a basic PC and get it working, and then add peripherals such as scanners, printers, and modems. Most people who build their own PC already have many of these peripherals anyway.

Having selected the components for your new PC it is time to add up the cost. This tends to be higher than you would expect, so it may be necessary to come up with some extra money or compromise slightly and choose some cheaper components. It is also worth looking through some catalogues and magazine adverts to see if you can find better deals on some of the components. It is essential to make sure that the components will actually fit together to produce a working PC. There are more options available than in days gone by, which means that there are also more opportunities for hardware incompatibility to creep in. Chapter 2 covers each component in detail, and should help you to avoid buying parts that do not properly match up.

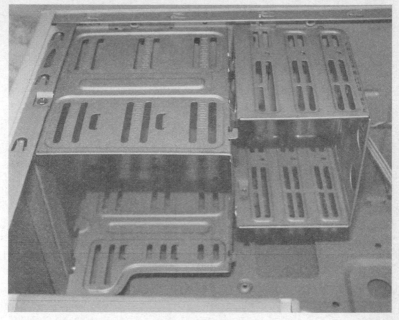

Fig.1.1 The case has bays for two sizes of drive

Assembly

Having obtained a complete set of parts it is then time to assemble the PC. Before starting to build the PC, look at the various components, including minor items such as cables and small pieces of hardware, and try to get a mental picture of how everything fits together. If you have a ready-made PC it is a good idea to open it up and look inside so that you can see how it fits together. The case you have bought should have two sizes of drive bays (Figure 1.1). The smaller bays take 3.5 inch drives such as a 3.5 inch floppy disc drive and most hard drives. The larger bays are the 5.25 inch variety and take CD-ROM drives, CD-ROM writers, etc. Usually one or two of the 3.5-inch drive bays do not have cutouts in the front panel. These are used for hard disc drives, which do not have to be externally accessible. There should be a large empty compartment in the case, and this is where the motherboard is mounted (Figure 1.2). The large box mounted on the rear panel of the case, usually in the top right-hand corner (as viewed from the front), is the power supply unit. This has mains input and (possibly) output connectors

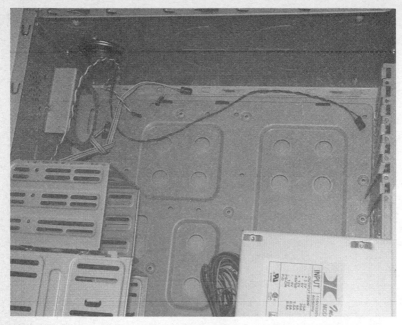

Fig.1.2 The empty area in the case is for the motherboard

on the rear, and a selection of power leads for the motherboard and the drives (Figure 1.3).

The case should be supplied complete with various small items of hardware (Figure 1.4), and it is bordering on the useless without them, so make sure it has the all important polythene bag of odds and ends. These small items of hardware include the screws that are used to fix the various drives into their cages, although suitable screws may be included with some of the drives as well. In days gone by it was often quite awkward fitting the drives into the case, with plastic guide rails being fitted to the drives before they were slid into place. The rails were then bolted to the case. This system now seems to be totally obsolete, and the drives are bolted direct to the inner structure of the case.

The motherboard has a socket for the processor, and two or more for the memory modules (Figure 1.5). Modern processors require a heatsink (a piece of finned metal) and a fan to prevent overheating. The heatsink and fan are normally sold as a single unit (Figure 1.6). Where possible it is better to fit the processor, heatsink and fan, and the memory modules

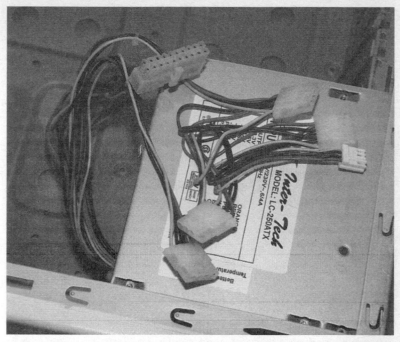

Fig.1.3 The power supply has about six output cables

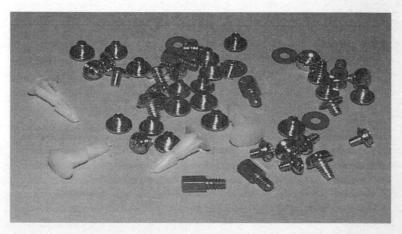

Fig.1.4 Small items of hardware should be included with the case

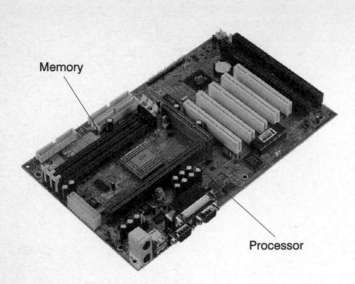

Memory

Processor

Fig.1.5 The memory and processor slots on an ATX motherboard

to the motherboard before it is mounted inside the case. Even with the largest and best designed cases there is relatively poor access to the motherboard once it is inside the case, so it makes sense to do as much work as possible while it is still freely accessible. Unfortunately, with some cases it might be difficult or impossible to slide the motherboard into the case with everything preinstalled, but where possible you should certainly do so.

There may be some DIP-switches (Figure 1.7) or jumpers (Figure 1.8) on the motherboard that have to be given the correct settings for the particular microprocessor you are using. These set the clock frequencies, processor operating voltage and possibly one or two other things as well. These should

Fig.1.6 A typical heatsink and fan   be set before the board is installed in the case because it is then much easier to see exactly what you are doing, and mistakes are much less likely to occur. It can be very fiddly indeed to set the miniature switches or jumpers once the board is fitted in the case. Not all motherboards are configured using switches or jumpers, and there is a strong trend towards so-called "jumperless" motherboards. These probe the processor to determine its type, and then set

Fig.1.7 A bank of eight DIP-switches

themselves up correctly without any guidance from the user. It is usually possible to override all or some of the settings manually if you do not agree with the default settings.

When the motherboard is finally installed in the case it must be held clear of the metal casing by mounting it on some form of stand-off. Without the stand-offs the connections on the underside of the board would simply short-circuit through the metal casing. The stand-offs might be moulded into the case or already installed, but they are usually in the bag of bits and pieces supplied with the case.

Fig.1.8 Some configuration jumpers

With the drives and motherboard in place it is time to start adding the cables. There are cables that connect the motherboard to the disc drives, and there will also be some leads sprouting from the front section of the case that connect to the motherboard. These provide functions such as the hard disc activity light and on/off switching. Depending on the type of power supply in use there will be one or two power leads to connect to the motherboard. The power lead on the processor's fan is connected to the motherboard, as is the fan for the case if there is one. The disc drives are not powered via the cable that connects to the motherboard, and each one must be connected to one of the power supply's power leads.

Fig.1.9 The blanking plates at the ear of the case

With an ATX motherboard and case there is no need to bother with wiring up the standard ports. The motherboard is fitted with standard connectors that can be accessed via cutouts in the rear of the case. The situation is different with an AT motherboard, whether it is fitted in an AT or ATX style case. The connectors for the two serial ports, parallel port, mouse port, and USB ports are mounted on the rear of the case, and then their flying leads are connected to the motherboard. Next the expansion cards are slotted into place on the motherboard and their mounting brackets are bolted to the rear section of the case. The appropriate blanking plates at the rear of the case (Figure 1.9) must first be removed to clear the way for the expansion cards. With more and more features being handled by the motherboard the number of expansion cards is often quite low on a modern computer. With the sound and graphics integrated with the motherboard it is not essential to have any at all, but most PCs utilize two or three cards. There are three types of expansion card, and therefore three types of expansion slots to accommodate them (Figure 1.10). The largest slots are the old ISA variety, which are now virtually obsolete, and not included on all motherboards. Most modern expansion cards are for the smaller PCI slots. The vast majority of modern motherboards have one AGP slot, which is used for graphics cards. However, PCI graphics cards are still available.

To complete the PC any final cabling is added. In most cases this just means adding the cable which connects the audio output of the CD-ROM drive to the appropriate input connector on the soundcard.

Fig.1.10 The three types of expansion slot

Cables and static

People contemplating building a PC for the first time are often worried about getting the cables connected incorrectly. In most cases this is simply not possible, because the cables are fitted with connectors that will only fit in the correct sockets the right way round. There are some cables where it is possible to make mistakes, but the instruction manual provided with the motherboard together with markings on the cables and connectors make it easy to get everything connected correctly. Provided due care and attention is used when fitting the cables there should be no problems. It is not a good idea to make a mistake, but if the worst should happen there is little risk of any damage occurring.

Another common worry is that of damaging some of the components by "zapping" them with static electricity. It is true that most of the components in a PC are vulnerable to static voltages, and that these voltages are quite common in normal environments. It is also true that there are numerous items of anti-static equipment available, which can virtually eliminate the possibility of components being damaged by static charges. Some of these anti-static devices are quite cheap, but many are quite costly.

For professional PC builders and service engineers it is probably worthwhile spending a fair amount of money on static precautions, as over a period they will be handling computer equipment worth many thousands of pounds. For the do-it-yourself PC builder it is not worth spending much money on this type of thing because the safety equipment

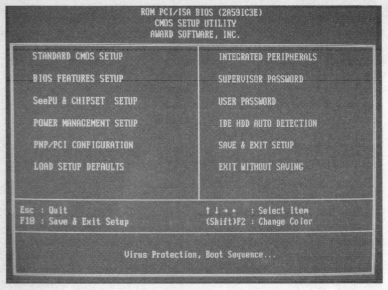

Fig.1.11 A typical main menu for a BIOS Setup program

could easily cost more than the components it is protecting. On the other hand, few amateur PC builders can afford to take no precautions and simply replace anything that is accidentally "zapped". Fortunately, it is not necessary to spend large amounts of money in order to protect the components. Some low cost equipment and (or) some improvised safety devices are adequate to ensure that your PC components will not be damaged while the PC is being built.

Setting Up

On the face of it, having built your PC it is just a matter of connecting the peripherals such as the monitor and mouse, and then switching on to see if it works. Unfortunately, it is not quite as simple as that. When you buy a new computer it is normally supplied fully configured with the operating system installed, and possibly even with some applications software already installed. It is then just a matter of connecting everything together, switching on, and computing away merrily. When you build a PC yourself it is necessary to configure it and install all the software yourself.

The configuration is done using the Setup program built into the PC as part of its BIOS (Figure 1.11). The BIOS is the basic input output system, and it is a program contained in a chip on the motherboard. It is sometimes referred to as the "ROM BIOS", because the chip that contains the program is a ROM (read only memory). A computer must always be running a valid program or it will

Fig.1.12 A lithium backup battery

crash, and the BIOS is the program that runs when you first switch on the computer. Its function is to do some basic checks on the hardware to ensure that the memory and processor are functioning properly, and to then run the operating system. The BIOS can be used by the operating system as an aid to handling the hardware.

A PC has some memory that does not lose its contents when the computer is switched off. This is normally in the form of CMOS RAM, which has a very low current consumption. As a result, a back-up battery is adequate to power this memory when the PC is switched off. In days gone by this battery was in the form of an ordinary battery pack that had to be changed periodically, or rechargeable cells that were charged up when the PC was switched on. These days the battery is usually a long-life lithium type that will last about 10 years and does not need to be replaced. It generally outlives the rest of the PC! It is usually easy to locate on the motherboard (Figure 1.12), and is a sort of giant size version of a "button" cell, as used In older cameras. The battery can actually be replaced in the unlikely event of it running flat or leaking. Incidentally, this battery also runs a clock/calendar circuit that enables the operating system to determine the time and date.

Originally the BIOS uses the CMOS RAM to store some basic information about the hardware, such as the amount of memory available, the main parameters for the hard disc drive, and the types of floppy drives installed. It still stores this information in the CMOS RAM, but it also uses it to hold numerous other facts and figures about the hardware. When your new PC is first switched on it is necessary to go into the BIOS Setup program to provide information about the drive types, to set the time and date, etc. There are also numerous other facts and figures that need to be set. A modern BIOS requires a large amount of information, and there is no denying that much of this information is highly technical. On the other hand, a modern BIOS is semi-intelligent, and it will set sensible defaults for most of the settings. It can also use probing techniques to obtain facts and figures about the amount of memory, the hard drive parameters, etc. In order to get the PC working it does not require a great deal of input from the user, and neither is a vast technical knowledge required.

Disc formatting

In days gone by it was necessary to do low level formatting of the hard disc drive, and then do high level formatting to suit the selected operating system. These days hard discs are supplied with the low level formatting already done, so it is only necessary to do the high level formatting. Whatever operating system you intend to use, it should have a formatting program that can handle hard disc drives. Actually there is a step needed ahead of formatting the hard drive, and this is to set up the partitions. By partitioning the disc it can be used as if it was two or more smaller discs. Even if you wish to allocate all the capacity to one partition, the drive still has to be processed using the partitioning software to produce this single partition.

Operating system

Just how difficult or easy it is to install the operating system depends on the particular operating system you select, and to some extent on the hardware in the PC. Getting a simple operating system like MS/DOS installed is quite quick and easy, but with a more modern operating system like Windows 98 or Linux it will take longer and is a little more difficult. Modern operating systems have quite sophisticated installer programs though, and to a large extent the installation is automatic. Installing an operating system on a PC is not quite as simple as loading a word processor or accounts program onto the hard drive, but it is not that much more difficult either.

With some operating systems and a modern PC you can boot from the installation CD-ROM. The programs on the CD-ROM may even handle things like partitioning and formatting the hard disc, leaving the user little to do apart from sitting back and watch what happens. With other operating systems, notably Windows 95 and 98, it is necessary to make a boot disc and boot from the floppy drive. The boot disc must include support for the CD-ROM drive so that you can run the Setup program on

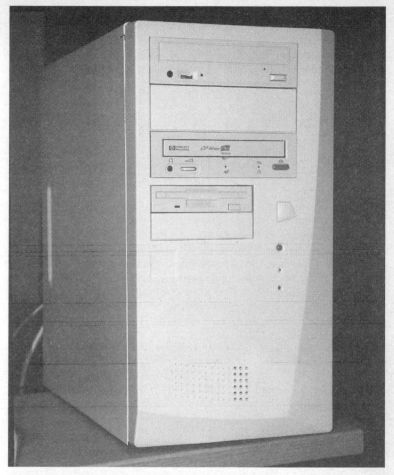

Fig.1.13 A completed Celeron PC in an ATX case

the installation disc once the computer has booted. It is then largely a matter of sitting back while the operating system installs itself on the hard drive.

Once the operating system is "up and running" it is time to install the applications programs and start using the new computer. Installing all this software and getting it set up correctly can be very time consuming. Where you have an old PC with the operating system and applications installed there are possible shortcuts to getting the new computer set up correctly. One of these is to simply use the old hard disc in the new computer, but it is likely that you will wish to use a disc having much greater capacity than that of the old drive. One way around this is to use the old drive as the boot drive, with a new drive being used as well to provide the extra storage capacity. This might not be as straightforward as you might think, because the new PC will have different hardware to the old one, and the operating system will require a substantial amount of reconfiguration before it will run in the new computer. It is possible to copy everything from the old drive to the new drive, but again, the operating system will have to be reconfigured before it will boot and run properly. This is not necessarily too difficult to achieve, and it is quite a popular option.

My preference would be to install everything "from scratch" even if it is very time consuming. When a PC has been in use for some time it tends to get cluttered up with all sorts of files that are no longer used, and the boot-up process often seems to slow down quite noticeably as a computer ages. Having built a new PC it is good practice to make a fresh start and only install those programs and files that you still need. This removes unwanted clutter from the hard disc drive and ensures that your new PC runs as quickly and smoothly as possible.

Points to remember

If you build your own PC to save money you can probably do so with careful buying, but do not expect to get a half price PC. If you do not shop around for the best buys it could actually cost more to build your own PC.

The manual skills involved in building a PC are not great, and no special tools are required. A medium size crosshead screwdriver and pair of pliers are all you should need, and no soldering is involved. Even so, PC construction is not for those who are completely impractical.

Provided you go about things slowly and meticulously the finished PC should work, and work well. There should be no significant difference in performance between a home constructed PC and a ready built PC of equivalent specification.

By building your own PC, funds permitting, you can have a PC that exactly meets you perfect specification. You should also learn a great deal about PCs and have plenty of fun as well.

The completed PC will require a certain amount of setting up before it is ready for the operating system to be installed. There is a trend towards having the PC automatically detect the processor type and adjust itself accordingly, so the amount of manual setting up may be minimal. Otherwise it is just a matter of setting a few switches or placing jumpers on the correct sets or terminals.

Some adjustments will be required to the BIOS, and these are performed via the built-in Setup program. The BIOS is admittedly highly technical, but to a large extent you can just leave the default settings. The user normally has to do little more than set the time and date, and provide some drive information.

Installing the operating system is not quite as easy as installing applications programs. On the other hand, modern operating systems have Setup programs that do most of the installation for you. It is necessary to provide some information when prompted, but little else is required.

With some operating systems it is necessary for the user to set up partitions on the hard disc and perform the high level formatting. This is not too difficult, and the operating system should be supplied with the necessary software to perform both the partitioning and the formatting.

No low level formatting is required with modern disc drives. The low level formatting is performed at the factory, and conventional low level formatting programs do not work properly will modern drives anyway.

There is no overall guarantee for the system if you build your own PC. If a component is faulty it is up to you to locate it and get it exchanged under the guarantee for that individual component. Locating faulty components is not usually too difficult, and in many cases the location of the fault is self-evident.

Components

Processor

All modern PCs are based on an Intel Pentium processor, or a compatible processor from another manufacturer. Pentium processors have additional instructions, but are basically just faster and more efficient versions of the 80486DX and earlier Intel processors in this series. The original Pentium chips ran at 60Mhz and 66MHz, and in most speed tests did not perform significantly better than the faster 80486 chips. Later versions used higher clock rates, fitted into a different socket, and had improved motherboards. This provided a boost in performance that gave much better results than any 80486DX PCs could achieve. The clock frequencies for these "classic" Pentium processors are 75, 90, 100, 120, 133, 150, 166, and 200MHz.

Although relatively recent, these processors are now obsolete and are not used in new PCs any more. Pentium processors with MMX (multimedia extension) technology replaced them. The MMX technology is actually an additional 57 processor instructions that are designed to speed up multimedia applications, but can also be used to good effect in other applications such as voice recognition. There were also some general improvements that produced an increase in performance by around 10 or 15 percent when using non-MMX specific software. These MMX Pentium processors were produced in 166MHz, 200MHz, and 233MHz versions.

These are now obsolete as well, and have been replaced by Pentium II and Pentium III processors. Pentium II processors have been produced with clock frequencies of 233, 266, 300, 333, 350, 400, and 450MHz. Currently only the 350, 400, and 450MHz versions are available, and even these

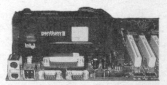

Fig.2.1 A Pentium II processor

are being phased out. The original Pentium processors were fitted onto the motherboard via a conventional integrated circuit holder known as

Socket 4. Those operating at 75MHz and above used an improved version called Socket 7. Pentium II processors look nothing like conventional processors, and in physical appearance they are like a cross between a videocassette and a memory module (Figure 2.1). They fit into a holder that is more like a PC expansion slot or holder for a memory module than an integrated circuit holder.

One reason for this change in style is that it potentially enables higher clock speeds to be utilized. Another reason for this change in style is that Pentium II chips are so complex that it is not possible to put the processor and cache memory on the same chip. Cache memory is high-speed memory that is used to store recently processed data. It is likely that this data will need to be accessed again, and having it available in high-speed memory ensures that it can be processed very efficiently when it is needed. In virtually all practical applications this substantially speeds up the rate at which data can be processed. Previous Pentium processors had some cache memory (typically 32k) on the chip, with a much larger cache of about 256 to 512k on the motherboard. These are known as level 1 and level 2 cache respectively. Level 1 cache is faster, but there are practical limits on the amount of cache memory that can be included in the processor. With the Pentium II chips it had to be omitted altogether, but a "piggy-back" memory chip included in the processor module provides a 512k cache. This memory runs at half the speed of the processor clock and not at the bus speed of the motherboard, which gives a substantial boost in performance. Due to the relatively large size of the level 1 cache no level 2 cache was deemed to be necessary. Hence there is no cache memory on a Pentium II motherboard.

The Pentium II is really a development of the Pentium Pro processor. This relatively unsuccessful processor was an improved version of the "classic" Pentium design, but when running Windows 95 software it often failed to provide much improvement over an ordinary Pentium chip. The Pentium Pro became overshadowed by the MMX Pentium processors, which proved to be an immediate hit with PC buyers. The Pentium Pro is no longer used in new PCs. The Pentium II has the additional MMX instructions, and slightly improved performance compared to an ordinary MMX Pentium processor. The 350, 400, and 450MHz versions are designed to operate on motherboards that operate at a 100MHz clock frequency and use fast memory modules. The earlier Pentium and Pentium II processors operate with 66 MHz motherboards and relatively slow RAM. This gives the 350, 400, and 450MHz chips a greater speed advantage over the slower versions than a comparison of the clock frequencies would suggest.

The Pentium III processor seems likely to take over from the Pentium II before too long, and the difference in price between the two is relatively small these days. The Pentium III has SIMD (single-instruction multiple data) technology, which is 70 new instructions designed to speed up certain types of software. These instructions are mainly aimed at high-speed 3D graphics and applications that include voice recognition. They are only of use with software that is written to take advantage of them. Like the Pentium II processors, the Pentium III has 512k of cache memory running at half the clock speed. At the time of writing this there are 450, 500, and 550MHz Pentium III processors, with 600MHz chips just starting to find their way into the shops. Faster versions should arrive soon.

Celeron

Intel has now abandoned Socket 7 technology in favour of the Slot 1 technology used for the Pentium II processors, and even higher tech Slot 2 processors are planned. The Intel processor for entry-level PCs is the Celeron, and in its original form it is basically just a Pentium II with the add-on cache omitted. This saves on manufacturing costs, but clearly gives a reduction in performance. The original Celeron did not exactly receive universal praise from the reviewers, and the absence of any on-board cache gives it a tough time keeping up with the latest budget processors from other manufacturers. Its performance is actually quite respectable, being around 15 to 30 percent faster than an Intel 233MHz MMX Pentium chip, depending on the type of software being run. Its performance is still well short of the slower Pentium II chips though.

The original Celeron processors were soon dropped in favour of a 300MHz version of the Celeron with 128k of on-chip cache running at the full processor clock speed. A 333MHz version and a succession of even faster chips soon followed this. Although at 128k the cache is only one quarter of the size of the cache fitted to Pentium II and III processors, the fact that it is on the same chip as the processor and operating at the same clock speed to some extent makes up for the smaller size. In fact with much software there is remarkably little difference in performance between a Pentium II processor and a Celeron operating at the same clock frequency.

The original Celeron processors used the same Slot 1 technology as Pentium II processors, and could be used in Pentium II motherboards. The current Celeron processors look very much like classic Pentium processors and are designed to fit Socket 370 motherboards. This reversion to old-style processor technology apparently helps to keep down the cost of these budget processors. The new Celerons will not fit directly onto a Slot 1 Pentium II motherboard, but it is possible to fit them onto this type of motherboard by way of an adapter.

Xeon

The Xeon is a form of Pentium II processor, and it is available with various cache options and clock speeds of 400MHz and upwards. Some previous Pentium processors can be used in dual processor systems, which, with the right software support, give significantly higher performance than equivalent single processor systems. The Xeon takes things further, and can be used in four processor systems, with eight processor computers planned for the future. It uses Socket 2 technology, and is therefore physically and electrically incompatible with Slot 1 motherboards. With its larger and faster cache than earlier Pentium processors, together with a 100MHz system bus, this processor is substantially faster than ordinary Pentium II chips. It is really intended for use in expensive network servers and not desktop PCs. It is beyond the budgets of most PC users and is not a processor that we will consider further in this book.

Non-Intel inside

The manufacturers of compatible processors have, as yet, not shifted over to Slot 1 technology or their own version of Slot technology. They have instead opted to develop Socket 7 technology as far as possible. The front runners in compatible chips are AMD and Cyrix. At the time of writing this Cyrix has been sold by National Semiconductors and is now owned by VIA, the PC support chip manufacturer. Development of these processors should therefore continue.

The first AMD processor for PCs was the K5, which was produced in 75, 90, 133, 150, and 166MHz versions. This chip was an alternative to the "classic" Pentium processor. It was replaced by the K6, which has the MMX instructions, and clock frequencies of 166, 200, 233, 266, and 300MHz. This was replaced by the K6-2, which was in turn superseded by the K6-2 3D Now! chip. This is a Pentium style processor that includes the MMX instructions, but it also has its own set of instructions that, together with the later versions of Microsoft's Direct X system, enable 3-D games to run at increased speeds. This processor requires a motherboard that can operate at 100MHz and fast memory modules. It is available with clock speeds of up to 475MHz.

The K6-2 has now been joined by the K6-3, which is basically just a K6-2 with 256k of on chip cache operating at the full processor clock speed. The cache on the motherboard operates as a level three cache incidentally. Versions having clock speeds of 400, 450, and 500MHz are available. With a substantial amount of on-chip cache memory running at the full clock speed the K6-3 provides a high level of performance. It is no longer the fastest AMD processor though, and that title goes to the Athlon (formerly known as the K7). This uses a slot

Fig.2.2 The AMD Athlon (K7) processor

rather than a socket and looks similar to a Pentium II or III (Figure 2.2), but it does not utilize Intel's Slot 1 technology. Instead it uses what AMD have dubbed Slot A technology. The K7 is available with clock speeds of 500, 550, and 600MHz, has 512k of level two cache, and operates with a system bus frequency of 200MHz.

The Cyrix equivalent of the AMD K6 is the 6X86 processor. This was produced in 90, 120, 133, 150, 166, and 200MHz versions. These chips cause a certain amount of confusion, because their speed ratings are not their actual clock frequencies. For instance, a 200MHz 6X86 processor is a 200MHz chip in the sense that it offers performance that is broadly similar to an Intel 200MHz Pentium. The actual clock frequency is somewhat less, and is actually 166MHz in this case. It has to be pointed out that how well (or otherwise) one make of processor compares to another depends on the type of software being run. Intel chips traditionally do well on floating point mathematics, but perform less well in other areas. If you are running a reasonably wide range of applications software, overall you are unlikely to notice much difference between equivalent chips from different manufacturers.

The original Cyrix processors are now obsolete, and they now produce processors that have the MMX instructions and these are the M2 series. These have clock frequencies of 166, 200, 233, 266, 300, and 333MHz, but only the two faster chips are currently available. Like the 6X86 processors, the speed ratings of M2 chips are their equivalent clock frequencies, and the actual clock frequencies are lower (225MHz or 233MHz for the 300MHz chip for example). As far as I can ascertain, at the time of writing this, Cyrix has released nothing beyond the 333MHz

Fig.2.3 A Cyrix 6X86MX processor and a Socket 7 holder

M2.   Figure 2.3 shows an old 200MHz Cyrix chip next to a Socket 7 holder, but all the Socket 7 and 370 chips look much the same. Figure 2.4 shows the numerous pins on the underside of the chip. Always handle Socket 7 and 370 chips with due care as they will not fit into the holder if any of the pins are buckled.

IDT and its Winchip are relative newcomers to the world of PC processors. The Winchip is intended to be a low cost processor for entry level PCs. It has the MMX instructions, and is produced in 150, 180, 200, 225, and 240MHz versions. At the time of writing this piece the rights to the Winchip are up for sale, and the future of these processors is uncertain.

There are other PC processors, but these are non-standard devices that integrate functions such as video and sound onto the processor chip. These require special motherboards that do not seem to be generally available. Some of these chips are intended for use in low cost PCs, but others are for use in embedded applications. In other words, for use in household gadgets, etc., that include a basic PC for Internet connection, or something of this type. This includes things like Internet television sets and the well publicised Internet connected "smart" fridge. It is advisable for the do-it-yourself PC builder to stick with mainstream processors that are used with standard PC components.

Processor advice

The range of processors currently available is a bit bewildering, and it can be difficult to decide which one is the most suitable. Unless money is not an issue it is probably best not to opt for the last word in PC microprocessors. When 66MHz 80486DX microprocessors became available they were only 33MHz faster than the existing 33MHz chips, but that 33MHz

Fig.2.4 Be careful not to damage the pins of a socket 7 processor

represented a doubling in speed. A 600MHz chip is 50MHz faster than a 550MHz version, but offers an increase in performance of less than 10 percent. Even with the more demanding applications software this will be barely noticeable. Programs that run slowly on a 550MHz PC will still run slowly on a 600MHz PC. Where there is a minimal difference in cost it might be worthwhile going for the slightly faster processor, particularly if you are running processor intensive applications, but otherwise it does not make economic sense to do so.

The main choice is between slot technology and processors that use conventional sockets. Socket 7 and 370 processors are generally much cheaper than the slot alternatives, as are the motherboards that accept them. They are probably fractionally easier for the home PC constructor to deal with as well. On the down side they offer what is likely to be somewhat inferior performance. If you really need high performance it will probably be necessary to opt for a Pentium II or III, or the AMD K7. Otherwise something like an AMD K6-3 or one of the faster Celeron processors should be perfectly adequate. It pays to bear in mind that much modern software will actually run perfectly well on a relatively slow PC. A 400 to 500MHz Celeron based PC does not provide the ultimate in performance, but it is still a fast PC that will run practically all mainstream software without "running out of steam".

Many people, quite understandably, would like their new PC to be as future proof as possible. In other words, they would like the PC to be easy to upgrade in the future so that it remains reasonably up-to-date at low cost. On the face of it slot technology offers better future proofing than socket technology, but matters are not really as simple as that. The fact that your PC has the right kind of slot or socket for a more modern processor does not necessarily mean that it will work properly with that processor. New and faster processors often need new and faster motherboards and faster memory as well. You can try to choose a set-up that can be easily upgraded, but do not be surprised if a future processor upgrade requires the motherboard and memory modules to be upgraded as well. I tend to concentrate on getting the quickest PC for the least money, and do not make future proofing a major consideration.

At the time of writing this piece the cheaper Celeron processors seem to be the best choice if a budget processor is required, and the AMD K6-3 (or possibly the K7) appears to be a good choice if something more potent is required. However, as Harold Wilson almost said, "a week is a long time in computing", and things change rapidly. It has almost become a matter of looking to see how many processor prices have been cut today, and checking to see how many new processors have been announced this week! It is really a matter of deciding on the processing power you require, and then looking for the best bargain at that power level.

Heatsink and fan

The original PC processors managed quite happily without any cooling system, but all modern PC processors are short lived unless they are kept cool by a heatsink and cooling fan. A heatsink is simply a piece of metal having fins that enable it to efficiently transfer excess heat from the processor to the air inside the case. The cooling fan improves the efficiency of the heatsink by ensuring that there is a flow of cool air over it. These days the heatsink and fan are invariably in the form of a single unit, and you do not buy them as separate entities. In fact processors are sometimes supplied as a sort of boxed set, complete with heatsink, fan, and fitting instructions, so you may not need to buy the heatsink and fan separately. In most cases though, they are not supplied with the processor, and must be purchased separately.

When buying the heatsink and fan it is important to realise that there are different sizes and types. A Slot 1 processor is a totally different shape to a Socket 7 type, and consequently needs a totally different heatsink and fan. Some Socket 7 processors generate more heat than others, and therefore need a larger heatsink. The safest way to buy the heatsink and fan is to obtain them from the same source as the processor and at the same time, preferably getting an assurance that the cooling system is suitable for use with the processor. Any company selling processors should be able to supply a matching heatsink and fan, and if necessary should be prepared to make amends for their mistake.

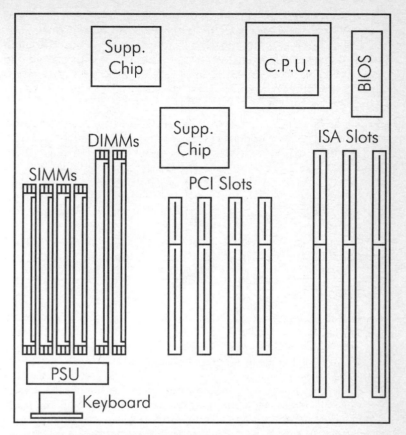

Fig.2.5 A typical AT motherboard layout

Motherboard

Having selected the processor it is then a matter of finding a suitable motherboard. It is important to realise that there are no universal motherboards that take all the current processors. A Socket 7 motherboard will not accommodate a Socket 370 Celeron or any form of slot processor. In fact a Socket 7 motherboard will not necessarily accommodate all the Socket 7 processors. When you find some likely looking motherboards it is essential to carefully check their specifications to ascertain whether or not they will accept the processor you intend to

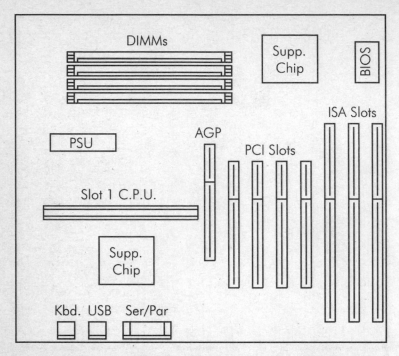

Fig.2.6 Typical layout for an ATX motherboard

use. It is worthwhile investigating the web sites of some motherboard manufacturers where you will find a lot of technical information on their motherboards. There are often charts to show the processors that are compatible with each board, and there may even be the full instruction manuals for the boards in downloadable form. Apart from helping you to select a suitable motherboard, reading through a few of these manuals can teach you a great deal about PC building and setting up the finished unit.

There are two main forms of motherboard, which are the AT and ATX varieties. The AT boards use what is basically the original AT layout, although modern AT boards are generally much smaller than the original design. Hence they are sometimes referred to as "baby AT" boards or something similar. ATX motherboards have a modified layout that puts the processor to one side of the expansion slots. Modern processors, when complete with heatsinks and cooling fans, tend to be quite tall and can obstruct several of the expansion slots. This prevents the slots

Fig.2.7 An AT motherboard for Socket 7 processors

from being used with the longer expansion cards. By moving the processor to one side this problem is avoided, and it is possible to use long expansion cards in any of the expansion slots. Figures 2.5 and 2.6 respectively show example AT and ATX motherboard layouts. Photographs of actual AT and ATX motherboards are provided in Figures 2.7 and 2.8 respectively.

This change in layout is not the only difference between the two types of board. They have different power supply requirements, with different types of power supply connector. Most AT boards have both types of connector (Figure 2.9). The AT connector is the one on the left, and the ATX connector is on the right. AT style boards are primarily designed for use with a power supply that has a conventional on/off switch fitted in the mains supply. An ATX power supply is switched on and off by way of a simple pushbutton switch on the case, which connects to the power supply via the motherboard. The point of this system is that it permits automatic control of the on/off switching. With Windows 98 for example, when the system is closed down the power supply switches off automatically. The monitor, assuming it is a reasonably modern type,

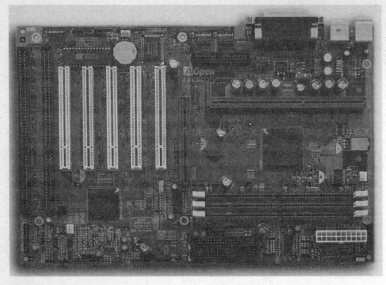

Fig.2.8 An ATX motherboard for Slot 1 processors

then goes into its power saving standby mode. This effectively results in the entire computer switching itself off when Windows 98 is shut down.

Another difference is the on-board serial and parallel port connectors of ATX boards. These are accessible via cutouts in the rear of the case, rather like the keyboard connector of an AT motherboard. In fact there is more than just the serial and parallel ports included in this group of connectors, and there is usually a minimum of two USB ports, a mouse port, and a PS/2 style keyboard port. Figure 2.10 shows a standard set

Fig.2.9 Modern AT motherboards have AT and ATX power connectors

of connectors, and Figure 2.11 identifies each port in the cluster. An AT motherboard has the larger 5-pin DIN keyboard connector incidentally. There may be other connectors included, such as a connector for a sound/MIDI port. This depends on

Fig.2.10 The standard ATX motherboard ports

whether or not the motherboard has any integrated peripherals.

The practical consequence of all this is that the two types of board require different styles of power supply and case. Actually, most modern AT motherboards are equipped for use in either type of case, and there should be no practical difficulties in using an AT motherboard in an ATX case provided the motherboard is equipped for the task. In fact an ATX case tends to be more commodious that an AT equivalent, making life somewhat easier for the do-it-yourself builder. It also makes it easier to upgrade the motherboard in the future, since there should be plenty of AT and ATX motherboards to choose from. With an AT case there is a dwindling number of AT motherboards that will actually fit the case. On the other hand, there is no obvious reason for using different types If you are building a PC "from scratch", unless perhaps you can obtain an AT motherboard and an ATX case at bargain prices. An ATX motherboard is totally incompatible with an AT case and power supply incidentally.

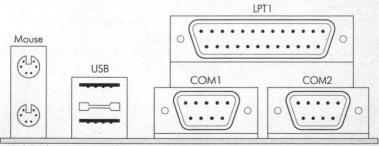

Fig.2.11 The standard ATX layout for the main ports

So which type of motherboard and case is the best choice? In the past the AT type has tended to be the most popular for do-it-yourself PC builders, probably due to the lower cost of both the motherboards and the cases. There has been relatively little difference in the cost of equivalent AT and ATX motherboards, but it was not uncommon for an ATX case and power supply to cost twice as much as an AT equivalent. Some price difference certainly remains, but is much smaller these days. Consequently, the more up-to-date ATX option is probably the one to go for. You will also have a much greater range of motherboards to choose from if you decide to use an ATX type.

Integrated functions

In recent years there has been a definite trend towards motherboards having integrated functions such as sound and video. Since motherboards that have these features do not cost a great deal more than those that do not they are an attractive proposition for those requiring a low cost PC. On the other hand, by using a motherboard of this type you might be "painting yourself into a corner". Sometimes any integrated functions can be switched off, but with many motherboards there is no way of disabling them. This could make it difficult or impossible to upgrade to superior sound or graphics should you wish to do so at some later time. Sometimes the motherboard has no AGP expansion slot, so there is no way of installing the latest AGP wonder video card even if the on-board graphics can be disabled. Also bear in mind that with many of these boards the main system memory is used by the on-board video and (or) sound circuits, so some extra memory has to be fitted in order to compensate for this. This is perhaps less of an issue than it used to be, as some extra memory costs very little these days.

Of course, if you simply require a good low cost PC, and will never need highly sophisticated sound facilities or the latest high speed 3D graphics, one of these integrated motherboards probably represents the best choice. They certainly seem to be gaining in popularity, and even some of the more upmarket motherboards now have integrated sound or graphics.

Case and PSU

Computer cases are normally supplied complete with a power supply unit (PSU). As pointed out in the previous section, there are two distinctly different types of case and power supply, for the two different types of motherboard (AT and ATX). Also as pointed out previously, the ATX is the more modern and versatile option, which is likely to be well worth any small extra cost. Whether you opt for an AT or an ATX unit there are four normal styles of case to choose from, and the most suitable style depends on the number of drive bays required and the space available for the finished PC.

A mini tower case is usually the easiest to accommodate in your home or office, but there will usually be provision for just two 5.25 inch drives and three 3.5 inch drives. This is sufficient for most purposes, since the majority of PCs have one 5.25-inch drive bay occupied by a CD-ROM drive, and two 3.5-inch drive bays taken up by the hard disc drive and a floppy drive. Even if a CD-ROM writer and a second hard disc drive are added, a mini tower will still have sufficient drive bays to accommodate them. The main problem with mini tower cases for the do-it-yourself PC builder is that they can be difficult to deal with. With a great deal crammed into their limited dimensions it can be difficult to physically get everything reliably fitted into place and connected together. Some mini tower cases are actually quite easy to work on, while others are a constant pain to deal with. Also, some mini tower cases are easy to use with some motherboards, but with others it is difficult to gain access to the memory sockets, the connectors for the disc drive cables, and this type of thing.

A midi tower case (Figure 2.12) is a safer option, with its extra 5.25-inch drive bay and what is usually a less crowded interior. The same is true of most desktop cases, but be slightly wary of some of the more compact desktop designs. These sometimes use unusual interior layouts that are not well suited to all motherboards. When building your own PC it is safest to opt for a conventional case that should take any standard PC components without difficulty. The top of the range cases are the full-size towers, and one of these is the best choice if you will be installing a range of drives, or may wish to upgrade the PC by adding more drives in the future. Apart

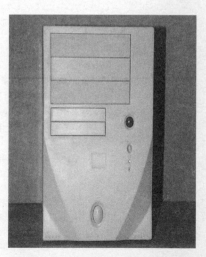

Fig.2.12 A MIDI tower ATX case

from having more drive bays, full-size tower cases are normally fitted with a slightly larger power supply that is well able to deal with extra drives, although at around 220 to 235 watts an ordinary PC power supply should not be found wanting in this respect.

Most cases have some or all of the drive bays removable, which can make life much easier. The 3.5-inch bays are often within the area of the

case occupied by the motherboard, and to some extent intrude over the top of the m o t h e r b o a r d . Particularly with the smaller cases, it can be much easier to fit the motherboard if the 3.5-inch drive bays are temporarily removed from the case (Figure 2.13). It can also be easier to fit the drives into the loose bays first, and then fit this whole subassembly into the case. The bays are much more

Fig.2.13 The 3.5-inch drive bays are normally removeable

accessible when they are removed from the case. Only choose a case that does not have removable bays if you are sure that it is well designed and enables the motherboard and drives to be fitted reasonably easily.

Virtual all PC cases have provision for a cooling fan, although many seem to be sold without this component actually fitted. Modern PCs generate significant amounts heat, due to the large amounts of RAM often used, complex processors that get very hot in operation, complex support chips on the motherboard that get hot, and so on. This tends to produce quite high operating temperatures inside the case, and can result in the over-temperature protection circuits on the motherboard coming into operation. This is most likely to occur on warm summer days when the air temperature inside the case is quite high even before the PC is switched on. If you are building a fairly high specification PC I would certainly recommend using a case that is fitted with a cooling fan, or adding a fan if it is not supplied as standard with the case.

Chipsets

When looking at the specifications for motherboards you will inevitably come across references to chipsets. These are the integrated circuits that provide various essential functions that are not included in the processor itself. In the original PCs these functions were provided by dozens of ordinary logic integrated circuits. Even though a modern PC requires much more help from the supporting electronics, there are normally just two or three support chips. Intel has manufactured various Pentium support chipsets, and these seem to be used on most Slot 1 and Socket 370 motherboards. However, other manufacturers make support Pentium chips, and these are to be found on various types of motherboard. They are particularly common on Socket 7 motherboards, because Intel does not produce support chips for modern Socket 7 processors. Here are brief details of the Intel chipsets.

FX   Early and basic Pentium chipset.

HX   Early chipset that is in many ways basic but is also fast. Provides dual processor support. Used for both Socket 7 and early Slot 1 motherboards.

VX   Early and basic chipset for Socket 7 motherboards giving SDRAM support.

TX   Improved chipset for Socket 7 motherboards which provides support for SDRAM, USB, and UDMA33 hard disc interface.

LX   First chipset specifically for Pentium II processors and Slot 1 motherboards. Provides dual processor, SDRAM, USB, UDMA33 and AGP support. Maximum memory of 512MB SDRAM, or 1GB EDO RAM.

BX   Effectively an improved LX chipset that supports 100MHz system bus and fast SDRAM. Up to 1GB or SDRAM or EDO RAM. Also supports 66MHz system bus for compatibility with 333MHz and slower Pentium II processors.

EX   Optimised for Celeron processor. Up to 256MB of SDRAM or EDO RAM. No dual processor support.

GX   Optimised for the Pentium II Xeon processors (i.e. 100MHz system bus processors) with no support for 66MHz bus.

NX   Support for up to four Pentium II Xeon processors and 8GB of SDRAM or EDO RAM. No AGP support.

ZX   Low cost chipset for Socket 370 Celeron processors. Supports up to 256MB of SDRAM.

810   For Socket 370 boards. Includes integrated 3D AGP graphics, plus software based audio, modem, and DVD capabilities.

Whether you opt for a board that uses Intel or non-Intel support chips it is advisable to select one that uses a modern chipset. There are usually plenty of bargain motherboards available, but most of these will not take modern processors. Those that can may only be able to do so by using the chips beyond their normal operating speeds, which could compromise reliability.

Memory

The first question to be resolved with memory is how much you should install in you new PC? For most software at present, 32 megabytes of RAM is quite sufficient. A few applications require much more than this, and programs that handle photographic images or other large bitmaps are particularly demanding in this respect. When handling large bitmap images in PhotoShop for example, it is recommended that the amount of RAM in the PC should be at least double the size of the bitmap. In order to handle scanned bitmaps of around 25 to 30 megabytes at least 60 megabytes of RAM would therefore be required. Fitting the PC with 64 megabytes of RAM should therefore give workable results, but 96 or 128 megabytes would probably give noticeably quicker and smoother running.

Bear in mind that large amounts of RAM can be needed in order to run several programs at once. In theory you do not need (say) 48 megabytes of RAM to multitask with two programs that require 16 and 32 megabytes of RAM. Somewhat less than 48 megabytes should suffice, because you are only running one copy of the operating system, and the two programs will share some resources. However, practical experience would suggest that 48 megabytes actually represents a realistic minimum in this situation.

Although memory has been very expensive in the past, it is currently quite cheap and putting large amounts of RAM into a PC is likely to be well worth the modest cost involved. Memory is like money, you know what, and hard disc space: you can never have too much of it. You do not hear people claiming that they have wasted money putting too much memory in their computers, but you do hear people expressing regret for not having specified more RAM when buying their PC.

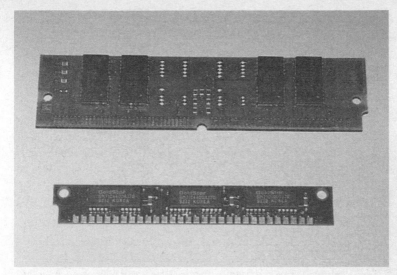

Fig.2.14 A 72-pin SIMM (top) and an older 30-pin type (bottom)

SIMMs

Until recently virtually all new PCs had their memory in the form of SIMMs (single in-line memory modules). A memory module of this type is a small printed circuit board, which is fitted with miniature DRAM chips of the surface-mount variety. The board plugs into a socket on the motherboard, and this set-up is like a sort of miniature version of the standard expansion slot system. The original SIMMs, as used in most 80386 and 80486 based PCs, have 30 pins. Although generally called 30-pin SIMMs, there are no pins and the connections to the device are via copper pads. The original SIMMs are now largely obsolete, and are only used for upgrading old PCs, and for certain soundcards and other peripherals.

The 30-pin SIMMs have been superseded by the 72 pin type, which are available in 4, 8, 16, 32, and 64 megabyte versions. Figure 2.14 shows both 30-pin (bottom) and 72-pin (top) SIMMs. Both types are available with or without the parity bit, which can be used to implement a simple form of error checking. With the old 30-pin SIMMs it was usually nine-bit wide modules having the parity bit that were required, but with 72-pin SIMMs, it is the modules that lack the parity bit that are normally used in

PCs. Two types of memory are available in 72-pin SIMM form. The original modules of this type were fitted with fast page memory (FPM), which is basically just ordinary DRAM chips. More recently an alternative form of memory called extended data output (EDO) RAM became available, which is actually just another form of DRAM. EDO memory usually gives somewhat faster performance than fast page memory, although the improvement obtained is unlikely to be more than about 10 percent or so. On the other hand, EDO memory no longer costs significantly more than the fast page variety, and is often significantly cheaper. It therefore makes sense to use EDO memory where possible, and some motherboards may only support this type of SIMM.

DIMMs

Although SIMMs are not quite obsolete, they are steadily being replaced by DIMMs (dual in-line memory modules) and are little used in new PCs. DIMMs look like outsize SIMMs, and have 168 terminals (Figure 2.15). SIMMs operate from a 5 volt supply, but the DIMMs used in PCs operate from 3.3 volts (like the input/output terminals of a Pentium processor). However, 5 volt DIMMs are produced. Fast page and EDO DIMMs are available, but it is SDRAM (synchronous dynamic random access memory) DIMMs that are normally used in PCs. Some PC motherboards will actually operate with fast page and EDO DIMMs, but as these modules are more difficult to obtain, slower, and usually more expensive than SDRAM, there would seem to be no point in using them. Buffered and unbuffered SDRAM DIMMs are available, but it is the unbuffered variety that is normally required for use in PCs. SDRAM DIMMs are available with capacities of 16, 32, 64, and 128 megabytes. Many of the early Pentium motherboards that accept this type of memory are incompatible with the larger sizes, so be careful if you are tempted to buy a "bargain basement" motherboard. If you have to pay high prices for lots of small memory modules the motherboard might not be such a bargain after all.

Currently there are two speeds of DIMM available, and these are now normally referred to as "PC66" and "PC100" DIMMs in catalogues. The PC66 DIMMs are suitable for use in motherboards that operate at 66MHz, whereas the PC100 DIMMs are suitable for bus speeds of up to 100MHz. It should perhaps be explained here that current processor technology has moved some way ahead of memory technology, resulting in the necessity to run the main system memory and the processor at different clock rates. This operates on the basis of having the processor operate

Fig.2.15 A 168-pin DIMM is much larger than either type of SIMM

at so many times the clock frequency of the motherboard. With a 450MHz Pentium II for instance, the motherboard operates at a bus speed of 100MHz with a multiplication factor of 4.5 to produce the 450MHz processor clock signal.

With a processor that operates with a 100MHz bus there will be no alternative to using PC100 DIMMs. With processors that operate with a 66MHz bus the motherboard will require PC66 DIMMs, but will almost certainly work with the PC100 type as well. Since these two types of memory module cost about the same, you may as well use PC100 DIMMs where possible. Should you upgrade to a faster processor at some later time there is a reasonable chance that PC100 DIMMs will be usable with the new processor, but little prospect of PC66 DIMMs being up to the task.

A few modern motherboards have a couple of SIMM sockets in addition to two or three DIMM sockets. This makes it possible to use EDO SIMMs with processors that will operate with a 66MHz bus, but there is little point in doing so unless you happen to have some SIMMs you wish to use in the new PC. EDO SIMMs will almost certainly cost a lot more than the same amount of memory in the form of PC100 DIMMs. Even if you do have some spare SIMMs, with the low cost of new memory it would probably be worth buying new DIMM memory anyway. This type of memory will give somewhat better performance than that provided EDO SIMMs.

Some of the newer processors and motherboards that are starting to appear require something beyond even PC100 DIMMs, such as PC133 and direct RAMbus modules. It is not really possible for me to comment on these new forms of super-memory because they are not generally available yet. If you are building a "state of the art" PC it is clearly essential to check the manual for the motherboard before buying the memory, so as to avoid obtaining the wrong thing. I would strongly recommend studying the manual for the motherboard before buying the memory anyway. The manual should make clear which type or types of memory can be used, the maximum amount of memory that can be fitted, and anything else that you need to know. As pointed out previously, many motherboard manufacturers have the manuals freely available for download on their web sites, and it is well worthwhile downloading and reading the manual for any motherboard that you are thinking of buying. You can then see whether or not it is likely to suit your requirements before parting with any money. It is also worthwhile checking through the "fine print" to see if there are any shortcomings that the advertisements for the motherboards have conveniently forgotten to tell you!

Keyboard and mouse

The choice of keyboard and mouse is a personal one, but make sure that you obtain a keyboard that matches the motherboard. AT motherboards are equipped with a 5-way DIN keyboard connector, but the ATX boards have the smaller PS/2 style connector (Figure 2.16). Many of the keyboards on sale are primarily intended for use as replacements for old PCs, and therefore have the AT style DIN connector. If you are using an ATX motherboard make sure that the keyboard you obtain has a PS/2 connector. Some keyboards have both types of connector, or an adapter that enables them to operate with either type of motherboard. In either case the keyboard is obviously usable with AT or ATX motherboards.

Modern computer rodents are for use with either a serial port or a PS/2 mouse port. It will not usually matter which type you buy because an ATX motherboard has a mouse port and two serial ports. I suppose that there is a potential advantage in using the mouse port because this avoids occupying one of the serial ports and leaves the greatest possible scope for expansion. On the other hand, serial ports are utilized rather less than was once the case, so one serial port left free could well be one more than will actually be needed! At one time mouse port mice had something of a reputation for causing hardware conflicts, but this mainly occurred where a mouse port mouse was used as a replacement for a serial mouse. This would sometimes cause problems with the mouse refusing to work properly. If the mouse was finally installed properly, sometimes another device such as a modem would refuse to work. Problems such as this are relatively rare these days, and did not normally occur anyway if a mouse port mouse was used from the outset.

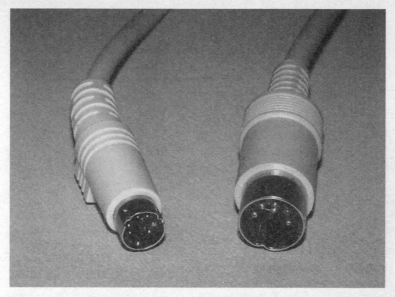

Fig.2.16 The PS/2 (left) and 5-way DIN (right) keyboard plugs

Floppy disc

In these days of huge data files, software distribution via CD-ROMs, and mass storage devices such as Zip drives and CD-ROM writers, the humble floppy disc drive is rather less important than it once was. It is still an essential part of the PC for most users, and installing the operating system can be impossible on a PC that does not have a floppy disc drive. Modern motherboards usually have support for all the normal types of PC floppy drive from 5.25 inch 360k units through to 2.88MB 3.5-inch drives. Probably most users will require nothing more than an ordinary 3.5-inch 1.44MB drive, but it should be possible to use something like a 5.25-inch 1.2MB drive if you need compatibility with old 5.25-inch discs. The only problem is that the older style drives tend to be relatively expensive, if you can actually manage to obtain one at all. A motherboard only has one floppy drive interface, but this can be used with one or two drives. There is no problem if you require (say) a 3.5-inch 1.44MB drive and a 5.25-inch 1.2MB type.

CD-ROM

In theory a CD-ROM drive is not essential part of a PC, but in practice the vast majority of software is now supplied on CD-ROMs, including most operating systems. The cost of most CD-ROM drives is such that there is little saving to be made by omitting one anyway. The cheapest and easiest type to deal with are the drives which have a standard IDE interface, or ATAPI interface as it is often called in this context. This is the same type of interface that is used for most hard disc drives, and a motherboard has two IDE interfaces. Each of these can handle up to two drives, making it possible to have a maximum of four drives. If you require something like two hard drives, a CD-ROM drive, and a CD-ROM writer, this set-up can be accommodated by the motherboard's built-in IDE interfaces.

Hard drives

As pointed out previously, most hard disc drives have an IDE interface that enables them to be connected direct to the motherboard. Hard and floppy disc controller cards are not needed with modern PCs. As the disc capacities have increased over the years it has been necessary for the operating systems and BIOS programs to be altered in an attempt to keep up with things. How well or otherwise large discs are handled depends on the operating system you are using and the motherboard. Assuming you are not building new PCs using old surplus or second hand components there should be no major difficulty in using high capacity drives. Where necessary, very large drives are usually supplied complete with any utility software needed to fully exploit their capacity. In fact hard drives are often supplied complete with quite a range of software designed to make it easy to install them in a new system or as an upgrade in an existing computer.

Drive modes

The IDE interface has received various updates over the years, but it has full compatibility with older drives. Any IDE hard disc drive should therefore work perfectly well with any modern motherboard. When dealing with IDE interfaces and hard drives, etc., you will inevitably come across references to the various IDE operating modes. In most instances you can simply let the system "do its own thing". The BIOS program should correctly determine and use the right mode for any device connected to it. However, it is worth taking a quick look at the various modes and the ways in which they differ.

PIO mode

A PIO (programmed input/output) mode is where the processor has direct control of the hard disc via one of the support chips on the motherboard. In order to place data on the disc or read it from the disc the processor must issue the appropriate commands to transfer the data between the disc and the computer's memory.

Master mode

In a master mode the microprocessor is not in direct control of the hard disc, but instead this task is handed over to one of the support chips. Obviously the processor still has to issue commands to the chipset so that it knows which data to access and where to place it, but the processor has little involvement beyond that. A Master mode is not inherently any quicker at transferring data than a PIO mode. However, it places less of a burden on the processor and can therefore provide a boost in performance in other respects.

DMA

This is direct memory access, and any mode where the chipset moves data between the disc and memory independently of the processor makes use of DMA.

There are five PIO modes numbered from 0 to 4 and the higher the number, the greater the maximum data transfer rate possible. There are three DMA modes numbered from 0 to 2, and again, the higher the mode number the faster the maximum transfer rate. These are the maximum rates for the four PIO modes and three DMA modes, but not all hard discs and PCs are necessarily capable of providing these rates. Also, not all drives can use the faster modes.

PIO Mode 0	3.3MB per second
PIO Mode 1	5.2 MB per second
PIO Mode 2	8.3MB per second
PIO Mode 3	11.1MB per second
PIO Mode 4	16.6MB per second
DMA Mode 0	4.16MB per second
DMA Mode 1	13.3MB per second
DMA Mode 2	16.6MB per second

Any reasonably modern hard disc drive should be able to support the faster transfer modes, but other IDE devices such as CD-ROM drives and other interchangeable disc systems may not. Bear in mind that there is no point in using a fast transfer mode with a device that can only accept or supply data at relatively low rates.

UDMA33/66

The vast majority of modern hard disc drives support Ultra DMA33 or even Ultra DMA66. These are developments that can only be implemented if the IDE interface on the motherboard and the hard drive both support them. They also need support from the operating system, and motherboards are often supplied with a suitable driver for Windows 95 and 98. As the names suggest, these modes provide transfer rates of up to 33 and 66 megabytes per second. Ultra DMA33 uses the same connectors and cables as a standard IDE interface, but the Ultra DMA66 interface requires a different cable. However, with a standard IDE connector an Ultra DMA33 hard disc can be used with an Ultra DMA66 interface on the motherboard, and an Ultra DMA66 hard drive can be used with an Ultra DMA33 interface on the motherboard. Of course, in both cases the drive only operates as an Ultra DMA33 type. It is only fair to point out that the potential increased speed provided by an Ultra DMA66 interface has yet to be matched by a hard disc drive that uses it. At the time of writing this the Ultra DMA66 interface offers a route to improved performance in the future, but does not provide a significant improvement with the current drives.

SCSI

Some up-market hard disc drives and even some CD-ROM drives do not use any form of IDE interface, but instead use a SCSI type. SCSI stands for "small computer systems interface" and is generally pronounced something like "scuzzy". This is really a general-purpose computer interface that can be used with a wide range of peripherals such as scanners and scientific instruments. It is used with the more expensive drives to provide faster data transfers, but with improvements in the IDE interface over the years SCSI drives perhaps have rather less of an advantage than they once did. If the ultimate in performance is essential, such as for a network server, a SCSI drive is still probably the best choice.

However, SCSI drives are not as straightforward to use as the IDE variety. Using a SCSI device has never been particularly easy, and matters have become more complicated over the years as new versions of this interface have evolved. Using a SCSI hard disc drive is certainly not something that could be recommended to first-time PC builders. Using a SCSI drive is not as difficult as it was in days gone by, where it was often necessary to use another drive to boot-up the system, and then use the SCSI drive as the main one once the operating system was set up successfully to recognise it. Motherboard and operating system support for SCSI devices is now much improved, and some motherboards actually have a built-in SCSI facility. It is worth considering one of these if you will be using the computer with a SCSI drive or other SCSI device. It is unlikely to make any great saving in cost compared to using an ordinary motherboard plus an add-on SCSI expansion card, but it can save a lot of hassle. There should be no problem with hardware conflicts when using a built-in SCSI port.

Other drives

These days it is not uncommon for PCs to have some form of interchangeable mass storage device such as a Zip drive, LS120 dirive, or a CD-ROM writer. The internal versions normally use either an IDE or SCSI interface, and the IDE versions are usually much cheaper and easier to deal with. There may be a performance advantage in using a SCSI version, depending on the innate speed of the device in question. In general these devices are handled much like a hard disc or a CD-ROM drive, but for LS120 and Zip drives there is often specific support available from the BIOS. In some cases it might even be possible to boot from one of these drives. Where necessary any driver software for operation with Windows should be included with the drive.

There have been problems in the past with interchangeable disc drives that the operating system considered to be fixed drives. The practical consequence of this was that the only way to get the system to use a changed disc was to reboot! Provided you use an up-to-date operating system and motherboard this sort of problem should not occur.

Video cards

One of the great strengths of PCs has always been that the video circuits are not built onto the main circuit board. This gives manufacturers the freedom to produce ever bigger and better video cards and the consumer the freedom to choose the most suitable card. You do not have to spend a large amount of money on the latest super-fast 3D graphics card if all you require is a simple 2D type. Neither are you restricted to simple 2D graphics when you really need advanced 3D capabilities. The video card you choose will obviously depend on the money available and the type of software you will be running.

You may have the choice of a PCI or AGP version of the selected video card. The original PC expansion slots used the ISA (industry standard architecture) interface. This was more or less the raw processor buses with some added wait states when an expansion card was accessed. These wait states were needed to slow things down so that the slower expansion cards could keep up. ISA expansion slots went through a certain amount of development, but are now largely obsolete and will be gradually be phased out. There are already motherboards that do not feature any ISA expansion slots, so if you wish to use an ISA expansion card in your new PC make quite sure that you obtain a motherboard that does have at least one slot of this type.

As PC technology advanced, the ISA slots proved to be too slow. They also made it awkward to implement new ideas such as "plug-and-play", and made it difficult to accommodate large numbers of expansion cards without hardware conflicts occurring. Eventually the PCI standard was adopted, and this removes many of the restrictions associated with ISA expansion cards. PCI cards use a different connector, and the port itself is totally incompatible with ISA cards anyway. A PCI slot is really a form

 of input/output port, and it does not operate direct onto the processor's buses like an ISA slot. While PCI slots are more than adequate for many purposes, they can limit performance when large amounts of data must be transferred. In

Fig.2.17 AGP (top) and PCI (bottom) connectors are totally incompatible

practice this mainly means when a video card is producing rapidly changing graphics. Hence the development of AGP slots for video cards. With "run of the mill" 2D video cards there seems to be little advantage in using an AGP interface, but for high performance 3D cards there is a substantial gain in performance. Note that PCI and AGP cards are physically incompatible (Figure 2.17), and electrically incompatible as well. An AGP video card is only usable with a modern motherboard that has an AGP expansion slot.

When building a new PC it makes sense to opt for the more up-to-date AGP version of a video card when both types of card are on offer. However, do not assume that all recent motherboards have an AGP expansion slot. With a current motherboard that is intended for some form of slot processor it is virtually certain that there will be an AGP slot. As far as I can ascertain, all Socket 370 motherboards have either an AGP expansion slot or built-in AGP graphics. Things are less certain with Socket 7 motherboards due to the lack of an Intel Socket 7 chipset that supports AGP. Other manufacturers have come up with Socket 7 chipsets that do provide AGP support, so most modern Socket 7 boards do have this feature. Be sure to check this point when buying low cost Socket 7 motherboards.

Monitor

In the past there were various colour and monochrome display cards that required different types of monitor. These old standards such as the MDA and CGA varieties are now obsolete, and the majority of modern PC monitors are incompatible with some or all of these old standards. Modern PC monitors are multi-standard types that can be used in the standard 640 by 480 pixel VGA mode, plus various super-VGA modes. The number of additional modes available varies from monitor to monitor, but at least the 800 by 600 pixel mode should be supported, and most monitors can also handle 1024 by 768 pixels. The higher resolution modes such as 1280 by 1024 and 1600 x 1200 pixels are not usually available on 14 inch and 15 inch monitors. Even if these modes were available, they would be unusable. With the Windows "big fonts" selected, menus, etc., would still be displayed too small to be really usable. In fact most PC monitors are barely usable in their highest resolution mode for this reason.

For each of the supported resolutions a monitor has a maximum refresh rate. This is simply the maximum number of complete scans of the screen that can be produced in one second. This is an important factor, because a low scan rate will produce a display that flickers quite noticeably. A display of this type is not unusable, but most users find them unpleasant to use for long periods. The minimum acceptable scan rate is a matter of opinion, but anything from about 70Hz upwards should be perfectly usable. I am reasonably happy with a 65Hz refresh rate, but at anything much less than 65Hz the picture flicker becomes very noticeable indeed.

Some monitors, particularly the smaller budget models, use interlacing when operating at high resolutions. Interlacing is where every other line is scanned on the first frame, then the missing lines are scanned on the next frame. Two frames (i.e. two scans of the screen) are therefore needed per complete screen-full. This method is used with low scanning rates that put less stringent requirements on the components in the monitor than fast and flicker-free scan rates. Ordinary television pictures are produced using interlacing incidentally. Although the interlacing helps to minimise problems with screen flicker, it does not eliminate them. If you will be using a computer a great deal it is probably best to invest in a monitor that can provide the resolution you require without resorting to low scan rates, with or without interlacing.

When looking at monitor specifications you will often encounter the term "dot pitch". In theory, the smaller the dot pitch, the higher the display quality is likely to be. In reality matters are not as straightforward as this, and two monitors having the same claimed dot pitch might actually give significantly different display qualities. The only way to judge the quality of a display is to try it out and make a subjective judgement.

The claimed size of the screen is something that is sometimes a bit over optimistic. Thankfully, some of the practices used in the past to inflate monitor sizes in specification sheets have now largely died out. If you buy a 14-inch monitor, you should not find that the diagonal measurement of the picture is actually about 11 inches. On the other hand, it will not be 14 inches either. Because the picture tube has rounded corners the usable picture size is somewhat less than the notional size. Some monitors give a larger display than others of the same specified size, but in general the actual diagonal measurement is about an inch or so less than the stated screen size.

These days virtually all monitors allow the horizontal and vertical sizes of the display to be adjusted so that it can be made to fill the screen. There should also be controls to enable the display to be accurately centred on the screen. Although you might expect two display cards operating in the same mode to position the display in more or less the same position on the screen, there can actually be quite large differences. Of more importance, the display can shift significantly when switching from one screen mode to another, and it can also expand or shrink. To avoid the need to readjust the controls each time the screen mode is altered, most monitors remember the control settings for each screen mode, and automatically switch to the appropriate settings when the mode is changed. Some video adapters are supplied with a utility that enables the card to be adjusted to suit the monitor for each screen mode. Again, the appropriate settings are used when the screen mode is changed, making it unnecessary to make any manual adjustments. Monitors normally have at least one or two controls that can be adjusted to minimise various forms of distortion, and in the case of larger monitors there are often several controls of this type.

Actually connecting the monitor to the video card should present no problems since all PC video cards and monitors use the same 15-way "D" style connector. The original PC monitors used a nine-way connector, but this became obsolete many years ago. In most cases there will be two ways of powering the monitor. The power lead supplied with the monitor will probably be a standard mains lead that enables the monitor to be powered from an ordinary 13 amp mains socket. It may instead be a type that enables the monitor to be powered from the mains output on the PC's power supply unit, or both types of lead might be included. Although most PCs have a mains output for the monitor, there are plenty that do not. ATX power supplies often lack this facility.

With an AT power supply the monitor supply output is obtained via the PC's on/off switch, so the monitor is switched on and off in sympathy with the PC. This is not a feature of ATX power supplies. When the PC is switched off the mains supply is still connected through to the monitor. However, modern monitors invariably have an energy saving facility that automatically switches them into a low power standby mode in the absence of a valid input signal. Strictly speaking the monitor is not actually switched off, but it is shut down to the point where it can be regarded as inoperative. Whether you power the monitor direct from the mains supply or via the PC probably does not matter too much, but where there is a choice I generally power the monitor by way of the PC.

Soundcards

PCs have a built-in loudspeaker, but this is driven by some very basic hardware that is really intended to do nothing more than produce a few simple "beep" sounds. For anything more than this a proper soundcard and a pair of active speakers is needed. Most soundcards do actually have built-in amplifiers, but they only provide low output powers and generally provide quite modest volume levels when used with passive speakers (i.e. speakers that do not have built-in amplifiers). The simplest soundcards only offer synthesised sounds, almost invariably produced using FM (frequency modulation) synthesis. FM synthesis gives adequate sound quality for many purposes, but wavetable synthesis is better for music making. This method uses standard analogue synthesis techniques, but the basic sounds are short bursts of recorded instrument sounds rather than simple waveforms from oscillator circuits.

Much more realistic results are produced using this method, although all wavetable soundcards seem to produce variable results. There are usually a few hundred different sounds available, and I suppose it is inevitable that some will sound more convincing than others. Modern soundcards can typically produce 32 or 64 different sounds at once, or in some cases much more than this. They are capable of reproducing quite complex music sequences, and in most cases sound reasonably convincing. Even the cheapest cards have the ability to record and play back in high quality stereo, and to play back pre-recorded sound samples (WAV files).

When dealing with soundcards you are likely to encounter frequent references to software and hardware wavetable synthesis. The hardware variety uses sound samples that are stored in a ROM on the soundcard, whereas software wavetable synthesis uses samples that are loaded from disc into the computer's main memory. Obviously the software type takes up some of the main memory, and less obviously it usually requires the processor to do more of the work. Since modern PCs tend to have plenty of memory and processing power this is less important than was once the case. Software wavetable synthesis has the advantage that it is possible to add or change sounds quite easily. This is normally only possible with hardware wavetable soundcards if they have some added memory, effectively making them a form of software wavetable card. Some soundcards offer the best of both worlds by having a mixture of software and hardware wavetable sounds.

In theory the hardware wavetable and simple FM synthesiser cards should be the easiest to install and use. In practice the software wavetable cards have drivers that largely hide the differences between the two types of card. Soundcards in general have a reputation for being awkward to install, and likely to uninstall themselves given half a chance. Certainly in my experience the most likely troublesome component in a newly constructed PC is the soundcard. Fortunately, the new PCI soundcards seem rather better than the old ISA variety.

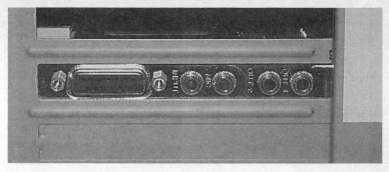

*Fig.2.18 The 15-way soundcard connector is for a combined
games controller and MIDI port*

MIDI

Apart from three or four audio input and output sockets, soundcards normally have a 15-way connector that is a combined MIDI port and game port (Figure 2.18). When used as a game port it takes standard PC joysticks and similar devices. When used as a MIDI port it enables music programs to operate with MIDI synthesisers, keyboards, sound modules, etc. However, note that standard MIDI cables have 5-way (180 degree) DIN plugs at both ends, and are therefore incompatible with the 15-way D connector of a PC soundcard. A special MIDI cable is needed to connect a PC soundcard to MIDI devices.

MIDI tends to cause a certain amount of confusion because most soundcards have two or three MIDI drivers. One of these is the MIDI port driver, and it will produce a Roland MPU-401 compatible port. This is the device you use in order to communicate with MIDI synthesisers, keyboards, etc., but does not get the soundcard itself to produce any sound. There will be one or two other drivers that produce virtual MIDI synthesisers. These can be used with software that has the ability to drive a MIDI device, and they get the soundcard to operate as a MIDI synthesiser. If the card has wavetable and FM synthesis there will probably be a separate driver for each type of synthesis. Additionally, there will be a driver for the joystick port. It is probably this proliferation of drivers that makes soundcards relatively difficult to install.

In the past PC soundcards were often equipped with an interface for a CD-ROM drive. The reason for this is simply that many peopled added a CD-ROM drive to their PC at the same time as they added a soundcard, since both of these items are required in order to run multimedia applications. Several CD-ROM interfaces have been used in the past, but only the ATAPI (IDE) and SCSI interfaces are currently in use on new drives. Some soundcards do still have a CD-ROM port, presumably so that they can be used as replacements or upgrades in an existing computer that requires an interface on the soundcard. Any port of this type is of no use with a new PC, so if possible switch it off, or simply ignore the port if it can not be deactivated.

Points to remember

You can not simply buy any motherboard and stick any processor on it. You must choose a processor and then look for a motherboard that supports the selected chip and has the features you require. Make sure the motherboard can handle a processor of the exact type and clock frequency you will be using.

Buy a matching heatsink and fan when you buy the processor. Some processors are actually supplied complete with a suitable cooling system, but most are not.

There are differences in the performance of similar motherboards from different manufacturers, but with modern boards these differences seem to be too small to worry about. Choose a board on the basis of cost, quality, and features.

No-name generic motherboards are significantly cheaper than those from well-known manufacturers. On the other hand, there is generally little or no support from the manufacturer with these boards, and it might be impossible to obtain BIOS upgrades. For the beginner at PC construction a board from a well-known manufacturer is the safer option.

If you buy an ATX motherboard you must use an ATX case and power supply. If you use an AT motherboard you can use an AT case or an ATX type.

Make sure the case is supplied complete with small items of hardware. It is of little use without them. The case and power supply should be bought as a single item, not separately.

A case that has removable drive bays is much easier to use than one where they are fixed. Small cases often give very restricted access to the interior, and medium or large cases are generally easier to deal with.

If you will be using a video card having an AGP interface make sure that the motherboard has an AGP expansion slot. Most do these days, but they are something less than standard on Socket 7 boards.

The old ISA expansion slots are gradually being phased out. If you have some old ISA cards that you wish to use in the new PC, make sure that the motherboard has sufficient ISA expansion slots to accommodate them. Some motherboards now have no ISA slots at all. Buy PCI expansion cards for the new PC and not ISA types.

The motherboard should be supplied with a basic set of leads for the drives, and with an AT board there should be cables for the serial and parallel ports as well. It can be expensive to buy these separately.

2   Components

Beginners would be well advised to buy hard drives and CD-ROM drives having an ordinary IDE (ATAPI) interface, and not SCSI types. IDE drives are much easier to use and these days they have quite respectable levels of performance.

An AT motherboard requires a keyboard having a 5-way DIN plug, whereas an ATX type requires a keyboard fitted with the smaller PS/2 connector. An ATX motherboard can accommodate a serial mouse or a PS/2 type, as can most AT motherboards.

Assembly

Protection racket

Those readers who are used to dealing with electronic components will no doubt be aware that most computer components are vulnerable to damage by static electricity. They will also be used to handling static-sensitive components and taking the necessary precautions to protect them from damage. Probably most readers are not familiar with these precautions, and I will therefore outline the basic steps necessary to ensure that no components are accidentally "zapped".

I think it is worth making the point that it does not take a large static charge complete with sparks and "cracking" sounds to damage sensitive electronic components. Large static discharges of that type are sufficient to damage most semiconductor components, and not just the more sensitive ones. Many of the components used in computing are so sensitive to static charges that they can be damaged by relatively small voltages. In this context "small" still means a potential of a hundred volts or so, but by static standards this is not particularly large. Charges of this order will not generate noticeable sparks or make your hair stand on end, but they are nevertheless harmful to many electronic components. Hence you can "zap" these components simply by touching them, and in most cases would not be aware that anything had happened.

I think it is also worth making the point that it is not just the processor and memory modules that are vulnerable. Completed circuit boards such as video and soundcards are often vulnerable to static damage, as is the motherboard itself. In fact most modern expansion cards and all motherboards are vulnerable to damage from static charges. Even components such as the hard disc drive and CD-ROM drive can be damaged by static charges. The case and power supply assembly plus any heatsinks and cooling fans represent the only major components that you can assume to be zap-proof. Everything else should be regarded as potentially at risk and handled accordingly.

Fig.3.1 An improvised conductive work surface

When handling any vulnerable computer components you should always keep well away from any known or likely sources of static electricity. These includes such things as computer monitors, television sets, any carpets or furnishings that are known to be prone to static generation, and even any pets that are known to get charged-up fur coats. Also avoid wearing any clothes that are known to give problems with static charges. This seems to be less of a problem than it once was, because few clothes these days are made from a cloth that consists entirely of man-made fibres. There is normally a significant content of natural fibres, and this seems to be sufficient to prevent any significant build-up of static charges. However, if you should have any garments that might give problems, make sure that you do not wear them when handling any computer equipment or components.

Anti-static equipment

Electronics and computing professionals often use quite expensive equipment to ensure that static charges are kept at bay. Most of these are not practical propositions for amateur computer enthusiasts or those who only deal with computers professionally on a very part-time basis. If you will only be working on computers from time to time, some very simple anti-static equipment is all that you need to ensure that there are no expensive accidents. When working on a motherboard it is essential to have some form of conductive worktop that is earthed. These can be purchased from the larger

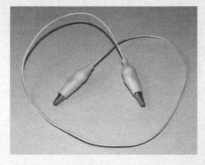

Fig.3.2 A crocodile clip lead

electronic component suppliers, but something as basic as a large sheet of aluminium cooking foil laid out on the workbench will do the job very well (Figure 3.1). The only slight problem is that some way of earthing the foil must be devised. The method I generally adopt is to connect the foil to the metal chassis of a computer using a crocodile clip lead (Figure 3.2). Crocodile clips are available from electronic component suppliers, as are sets of made-up leads. The ready-made leads are often quite short, but several can be clipped together to make up a longer lead. The computer that acts as the earth must be plugged into the mains supply so that it is earthed via the mains earth lead. The computer should be switched off, and the supply should also be switched off at the mains socket. The earth lead is never switched, and the case will remain earthed even when it is switched off.

If you wish to make quite sure that your body remains static-free, you can earth yourself to the computer by way of a proper earthing wristband. This is basically just a wristband made from electrically conductive material that connects to the earth via a lead and a high value resistor. The resistor does not prevent any static build-up in your body from leaking away to earth, but it will protect you from a significant shock if a fault should result in the earthing point becoming "live". If you do not want to go to the expense of buying a wristband, a simple but effective alternative is to touch the conductive worktop or the metal chassis of the computer from time to time. This will leak away any gradual build-up of static electricity before it has time to reach dangerous proportions. Again, the computer must be connected to the mains supply, but it should be switched off and the mains supply should be switched off at the mains outlet.

That is really all there is to it. Simply having a large chunk of earthed metal (in the form of the computer case) near the work area helps to discourage the build-up of any static charges in the first place. The few simple precautions outlined previously are then sufficient to ensure that there is no significant risk to the components. Do not be tempted to simply ignore the dangers of static electricity when handling computer components. When building electronic gadgets I often ignore static precautions, but I am dealing with components that cost a matter of pence each. If one or two of the components should be zapped by a static charge, no great harm is done. The same is not true when dealing with computer components, some of which could cost in excess of a hundred pounds.

Anti-static packing

One final point is that any static sensitive components will be supplied in some form of anti-static packaging. This is usually nothing more than a plastic bag that is made from a special plastic that is slightly conductive.

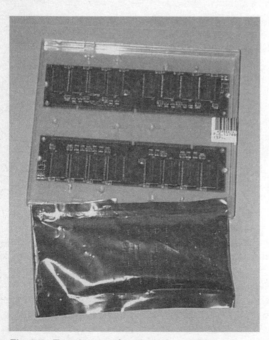

Processors and memory modules are often supplied in something more elaborate, such as conductive plastic clips and boxes. There is quite a range of anti-static packaging currently in use, and Figure 3.3 shows a couple of examples.

Although it is tempting to remove the components from the packing to have a good look at them, try to keep this type of thing to a minimum. When you do remove the components from the bags make sure that you and the

Fig.3.3 Two forms of anti-static packing

bags are earthed first. Simply touching the earthed chassis of a computer while holding the component in its bag should ensure that everything is charge-free. Make sure that you always handle the components in an environment that is free from any likely sources of static charges. There will then be a minimal risk of any damage occurring.

Case

Having set up any necessary anti-static precautions the next task is to get the case ready for assembly to begin. Unless you obtain one of the more exotic cases there should be no difficulty in opening the case. Removing four or six screws at the rear of the case should release the outer casing. Look carefully to see which screws actually hold the outer casing in position, or you will find that you have removed the power supply instead! With an AT case the outer casing is normally in one piece which forms the top and two sides of the case. The basic design of an ATX case is somewhat different, and two separate side panels are released when the screws at the rear of the case are removed. The lid of the case forms part of the main structure and is left in place. Figure 3.4 shows an ATX case with one side panel removed. With most ATX cases you only need to remove the left-hand side panel (as viewed from the front) in order to do most of the assembly work. The other side panel will probably have to be removed in order to mount the 5.25-inch drives properly.

Inside the case there should be a mains lead fitted with suitable connectors at both ends. The end that connects to the computer normally has a standard IEC plug,

Fig.3.4 Removing one side panel gives good access to an ATX case

Fig.3.5 *The metal plates supplied with an ATX case*

as used for most mains powered gadgets these days. There will also be various items of hardware, and if you are using an ATX case there will probably be two or three metal plates with various holes stamped in them (Figure 3.5). If you are using an AT motherboard these will not be needed, but they should be kept for possible use in the future.

As pointed out in the previous chapters, an ATX motherboard has the standard ports actually fitted on the board, and the connectors for these ports are accessed via a cutout in the case. However, as supplied most PC cases do not have the necessary cutouts in the rear of the case. This is because these cases are designed for use with AT or ATX motherboards, and initially they are set up for use with AT boards. If you look at the case where the cutouts

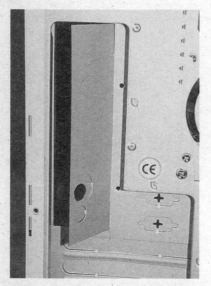

Fig.3.6 *Removing the port cover plate from an ATX case*

should be you will probably find that there is a metal panel instead. This panel will be largely cut from the case, and will only be held in place by two or three thin pieces of metal. This approach to things is used a great deal with modern computer cases, and it is a simple way of having optional cutouts. Simply leave things as they are if a cutout is not needed, or remove the piece of metal if a cutout is needed. Removing an unwanted panel is not difficult, and it is just a matter of pressing it with your finger to break one side free from the case (Figure 3.6). Then the panel is waggled backwards and forwards a few times until the fingers of metal securing it to the case fatigue and break.

There may be some rough edges produced where the metal fatigues and breaks. It is tempting to use a miniature file to rectify this, but filing or cutting a PC case using a saw is not something to be recommended. The problem is simply that the small metal fragments produced are difficult to thoroughly clean from the case, and they are also good at producing short-circuits if they get onto any of the circuit boards. If there are any dangerously sharp edges they must be removed, but otherwise do not bother. If you do have to file away any sharp edges try to thoroughly clean away any swarf. A damp rag does the job quite well, but the sticky side of adhesive tape or some Bostik Blu-Tack are probably the most effective ways of mopping up the swarf.

Having removed the panel you can simply leave a large hole in the rear panel, but one of the plates supplied with the case should match up properly with the connectors on the motherboard. Much neater results will be produced if this is bolted in place on the rear panel (Figure 3.7). Depending on the ports fitted to the motherboard, you may have to press out one or two small pieces of metal from the panel to make it match the connectors on the motherboard. This is not difficult, and is done in the same way as removing the main panel from the rear of the case.

Fig.3.7 The new port cover plate installed on an ATX case

If you are using an AT motherboard in an ATX case there should be little adjustment needed to the metalwork of the case. Probably the only thing you will have to do is remove the small piece of metal that partially covers the entrance for the keyboard connector. As supplied this will have a small opening to accept a PS/2 keyboard plug, but with the piece of metal that partially covers the cutout removed the cutout will be big enough for an ordinary DIN style keyboard connector.

Stand-offs

The next task is to install the stand-offs on which the motherboard will be mounted. It is possible that these will be built into the chassis, or that they will already be fitted to the chassis. This is unlikely though, and the first part of the assembly process is to fit the stand-offs to the chassis. If you look at the mounting holes in the motherboard and those in the chassis you will find that there are many more in the chassis. This is simply because the case is normally designed to take various types of motherboard, old and new. Some of the holes in the chassis probably have no relevance to any modern motherboards, and others will probably not be relevant to the particular board you are using.

The only sure way of telling which holes in the chassis should be fitted with stand-offs is to place the motherboard in position inside the case. With most cases it should be possible to fit the motherboard in place without any difficulty, but with some of the smaller cases it will be necessary to remove the 3.5-inch drive bay. Do not flex the board or use force to get it into position, as this could easily damage it beyond repair. Methods of fixing the drive bay cages vary somewhat, but it usually involves nothing more than undoing one or two screws and sliding the cage out from the main assembly. It often takes a fair amount of force to get the cage free. Once the motherboard is inside the case it can be moved around until all the holes in the board match up with holes in the case. Make a careful note of which holes in the case should be fitted with stand-offs, making a quick sketch if necessary.

It is possible that there will be some holes in the motherboard that have no counterparts in the case. This is actually quite normal with an AT motherboard, which normally has two or three mounting holes along the front edge but no matching mounting points in a modern case. The extra holes can simply be left unused, and provided there are at least four mounting points spread well across the board it should be held in place adequately. A check through odds and ends of hardware supplied with the board will probably throw up a few plastic stand-offs that can be fitted into the underside of the motherboard, but have no provision for fixing to the chassis (Figure 3.8). These stand-offs are simply pushed into a mounting hole on the underside of the motherboard, and they can be used in any holes that have no counterparts in the case. They will avoid any tendency for the board

Fig.3.8 Two plastic stand-offs

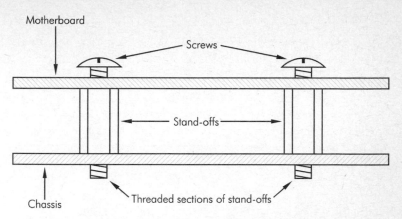

Motherboard

Screws

Stand-offs

Chassis

Threaded sections of stand-offs

Fig.3.9 The most common form of stand-off for motherboards

to droop and possibly short circuit to the case. They will also effectively stiffen the board, reducing the risk of any damage occurring when fitting any expansion cards that need firm pushes to slot them into place.

There are several types of stand-off used with motherboards. Probably the most common stand-off at present is the hexagonal type that has a threaded section at the base which screws into the threaded holes in the chassis. The motherboard is then bolted to the stand-offs (Figure 3.9). These should be screwed quite firmly into the chassis, but with computers it is not a matter of tightening everything as hard as you can. In order to avoid sheared threads you should tighten things enough to prevent them from easily coming apart again, but no more. In the absence of a suitable nut-driver for the stand-offs a pair of pliers should enable them to be tightened properly.

A similar type of stand-off is fixed in place by a screw, as in Figure 3.10. There are also plastic types that clip into the motherboard and slide into cutouts in the chassis, and this type is also depicted in Figure 3.10. These operate in conjunction with one or two metal stand-offs that enable the board to be bolted in place, and provide an electrical connection from the earth rail of the motherboard to the case. The slide-in approach can be a bit awkward in practice with some of the stand-offs tending to buckle under the board rather than sliding nicely into place. If necessary, slide the motherboard back out again and try again, and do not simply leave the board supported by buckled stand-offs. They may fall out of position and permit the board to short-circuit to the case. There are

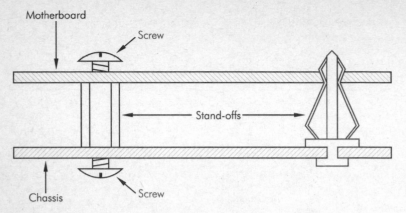

Fig.3.10 Two more common forms of stand-off

other types of stand-off in use, but they are mostly variations on the types described here. It should not be too difficult to work out how other types of stand-off are used.

Be careful not to fit metal stand-offs to the chassis at any points where there are no matching mounting holes in the motherboard. Doing so could result in connections on the underside of the board being short-circuited to the case. Once the stand-offs are in place the motherboard should be mounted inside the case to ensure that everything fits correctly. When you have established that everything fits correctly the motherboard should be removed so that the processor and memory can be installed, and (where appropriate) the motherboard can be configured via the DIP-switches and jumpers.

Configuration

Some motherboards do not require any configuration at this stage of the proceedings, but are instead configured using the BIOS Setup program. In fact most of these boards configure themselves using probing techniques to determine what processor is fitted, and manual configuration is only needed if you do not agree with the default settings for some reason. If you are not using one these "jumperless" boards it will be necessary to use DIP-switches or jumpers to set up the board to suit the processor. Manuals for pieces of electronic equipment and computer software tend to get ignored, and are only read as a last resort.

This is not an option when dealing with motherboards, and it is essential to read through the manual and constantly refer to it for vital pieces of information. You will certainly need to study the instruction manual for details of how to set it up to suit the particular processor you are using.

The parameters that are set via the jumpers or switches depend on the type of motherboard in use. With a Socket 7 motherboard there are usually several things that need to be set up correctly. The processor and motherboard clock speeds must be set, and the two are linked. The correct clock rate for the motherboard is set, and then a multiplier is used to produce the required clock frequency. As a couple of examples, a Celeron processor operating at 500MHz with a 66MHz motherboard clock frequency would require a multiplier value of 7.5 (66 x 7.5 = 495). A Pentium III operating at 500MHz with a 100MHz bus frequency would require a multiplier value of five (100 x 5 = 500). As will be apparent from the first of these examples, the mathematics is not always perfect. In the Celeron example, the actual processor clock frequency will be slightly lower than its nominal value, or the motherboard bus speed will be fractionally higher (66.66MHz instead of 66MHz). It does not really matter which, and there will be no noticeable difference in performance between clock rates of 495 and 500MHz.

Cyrix clock rates

There is a slight complication with the processor frequency for the Cyrix chips in that their actual clock frequencies are lower than the name of the processor would suggest. Also, there can be more than one version of the chip, with each version requiring a different clock frequency. For example, the 300MHz Cyrix chip has been produced in versions that require 225 and 233MHz clock frequencies. The 300MHz figure is a sort of Intel equivalent rating, and takes into account the fact that the Cyrix processor needs fewer clock cycles to perform some instructions. The actual performance of PC processors depends on the software being run, so any equivalent of this type has to be taken with the proverbial "pinch of salt". Anyway, the actual clock frequency is either 225MHz (75MHz x 3) or 233MHz (66MHz x 3.5). Although the 233MHz version might be expected to outperform the 225MHz processor, the higher system bus frequency of the 225MHz chip compensates for the lower processor clock frequency. The two versions therefore have very similar levels of performance.

Obviously there is the potential for confusion with processors that are available in more than one version. How do you know which version of

*Fig.3.11 A Cyrix processor marked
with the system clock
frequency and multiplier*

the chip you have? To avoid mistakes these processors have the bus frequency and multiplier marked on the top of the chip, and the correct core voltage is usually indicated as well (Figure 3.11). Always set up the motherboard to suit the clock frequency and multiplier indicated on the processor itself, even if the bus frequency and multiplier stated in the motherboard manual are different. It will always be the multiplier value and bus frequency on the chip itself that will be correct.

Core voltage

With a Socket 7 board it is also necessary to set the processor core voltage. Conventionally logic circuits operate from a 5-volt supply, but in order to get the highest possible performance it is common practice for other supply voltages to be used in parts of the computer. Memory circuits and some sections of the processor often operate at 3.3 volts, and the main processor circuits often work at a somewhat lower voltage. It is this second voltage, or core voltage that is set via the jumpers or DIP-switches. The instruction manual for the motherboard should give the correct settings for all the usable processors. It is common for the correct core voltage to be marked on the top surface of the processor, particularly with non-Intel devices. If the marked core voltage is different to the one indicated on the chip itself, set up the motherboard to provide the voltage indicated on the chip.

There may be other settings to make, but these additional parameters vary a lot from one motherboard to another. One virtually standard feature is a jumper that enables the CMOS memory to be disconnected from the backup battery. By default this should be set so the board functions normally, with the backup battery ensuring that the BIOS is free from amnesia, with the correct drive parameters, etc., being used each time the computer is switched on. Setting this jumper to the "off" position for a few minutes wipes the CMOS memory of all its contents. With the jumper restored to the "on" setting the computer is able to function again, but it is a matter of starting "from scratch" with the CMOS memory settings.

In effect, this jumper provides a means of resetting the CMOS memory. This would be probably only be necessary if someone started to use the password facility and then forgot his or her password. The only way of getting the computer to boot if this happens is to clear the current set-up from memory. The next time the computer is started it uses the default settings, which means that it starts up without implementing the password facility. Unless there is a good reason to do so, it is best not to use any BIOS password facility. Note that it is not necessary to clear the CMOS memory in this way if you manage to make a complete mess of the BIOS settings. From within the BIOS Setup program it is usually possible to revert to one or two sets of default settings, and then do any necessary "fine tuning".

There can be other jumpers or DIP-switches to set such things as the supply voltage for the memory modules, to disable the built-in audio system, and this type of thing. You really have to read the manual for the motherboard to determine what jumpers or DIP-switches have to be set up correctly, if any. The modern trend is towards as much as possible being set using auto-detection methods, or via the BIOS Setup program. Many motherboards only have one switch or jumper that can be used to power-down the CMOS memory.

Setting up

Actually setting any jumpers or switches should not give any major problems. There are two types of jumper, which are the straightforward on/off type and the two-way variety. The on/off type has two pins and you fit the jumper over the pins to connect them together ("on") or do not fit the jumper at all ("off"). This simple scheme of things is shown in Figure 3.12(a). It is common practice to fit the jumper on one of the pins to provide the "off" setting. If you should need to change the setting at a later time you then know exactly where to find the jumper. The jumpers are minute and are likely to get lost if you store them somewhere other than on the motherboard. The second type of jumper block has three pins, and the jumper is used to connect the middle pin to one of the outer pins (Figure 3.12(b)). The jumper is connecting together two pins, as before, and the jumpers are exactly the same whether they are used on a two-pin block or a three-pin type.

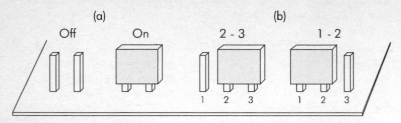

Fig.3.12 *The two types of jumper normally used on motherboards*

Fig.3.13 *The "ON" marking on a DIP-switch*

DIP-switches are normally in blocks of four or eight switches, but not all the switches in a block will necessarily be utilized. They are a form of slider switch, and are more or less a miniature version of the switches often used in small electronic gadgets such as cassette recorders and personal stereo units. The block of switches is marked with "on" and (or) "off" legends (Figure 3.13) to make it clear which setting is which.

The motherboard's instruction manual normally includes a diagram showing the correct switch or jumper settings for a given processor. There is a slight problem here in that these diagrams are open to misinterpretation. In the two examples of Figure 3.14, which pins do the jumpers connect and which switches are in the "on" position? My guess would be that the black blocks represent the jumpers and the control knobs on the switches, but there is no way of telling for sure without some further assistance. The manual should provide this assistance in the form of another diagram showing exactly how the switch or jumper setting diagrams should be interpreted. These diagrams will be

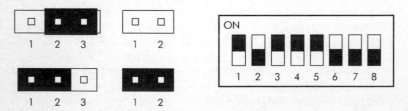

Fig.3.14 *Some switch and jumper diagrams are clearer than others*

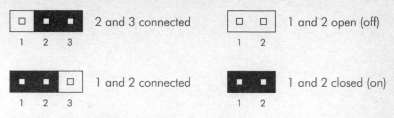

2 and 3 connected

1 and 2 open (off)

1 and 2 connected

1 and 2 closed (on)

Fig.3.15 An explanatory diagram for jumper settings

something like Figure 3.15 and 3.16. Never rely on guesswork when setting jumpers and DIP-switches. Mistakes are unlikely to result in any damage, but it is not worth taking the risk. Carefully study the instruction manual for the motherboard and get things right first time. Some instruction manuals provide charts listing the

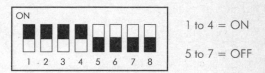

1 to 4 = ON

5 to 7 = OFF

Fig.3.16 An explanatory diagram for DIP-switches

correct settings for various processors, and these are often easier to use than the diagrams. Where you have the option I would certainly recommend using the charts.

Processor

Once any necessary configuring of the board has been completed the processor can be fitted into its socket. This is much the same for Socket 7 and Socket 370 processors, which are conventional integrated circuits. Both of these sockets are forms of ZIF (zero insertion force) socket. Conventional integrated circuit holders, even when used with integrated circuits that have only a few pins, are something less than easy to use. It is often quite difficult to squeeze the integrated circuits into them. The Socket 7 and Socket 370 chips have literally hundreds of pins. In fact the "370" in the Socket 370 name refers to the number of pins. Getting a chip of this size into a holder could be bordering on the impossible, but the situation is greatly eased by the use of ZIF sockets. The holder has a lever that is raised to the vertical position in order to open the socket (Figure 3.17). The lever normally has to be pulled outwards slightly in order to unlock it before it can be raised. With the socket open the

Socket Locked

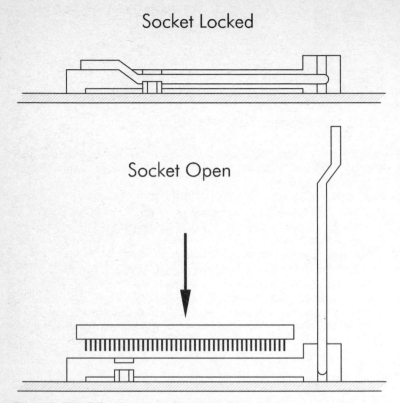

Socket Open

Fig.3.17 The ZIF socket is opened by raising the lever

processor should simply drop into place without any difficulty. Returning the lever to its original position then locks the processor in place.

The processor must be fitted with the correct orientation, and with modern socket processors it impossible to fit a processor the wrong way round. If you look at the socket you will find that there are three corners that have provision for a pin on the processor, and one that does not (Figure 3.18). It is this missing hole in the socket that prevents the processor from fitting into it unless the processor has the correct orientation. If you look at the upper surface of the processor you will find a dot in one corner, and that corner of the casing will probably be chamfered as well (Figure 3.19). If you match that corner of the chip with the missing hole in the socket, the processor should drop easily into place.

Fig.3.18 *To make it impossible to fit the processor the wrong way round, one hole is omitted from the socket (seen here in the bottom left-hand corner)*

Fig.3.19 *A dot on the top surface of the processor, together with a chamfered corner, indicate the position of the missing pin and the correct orientation for the chip*

Slot 1

Slot processors do not use conventional integrated circuit holders, but instead fit into a socket that is more like a holder for memory modules or an ordinary PCI expansion slot. The slot style processors are often referred to as "cartridges", and in appearance they are more like some form of video cartridge than a conventional integrated circuit. In common with PCI slots and DIMM holders, there is an off-centre break in the rows of connections that makes way for a polarising key in the casing of the processor (Figure 3.20). This makes it easy to see which way round the processor should be inserted into the slot, and makes it impossible to fit it the wrong way round. A cartridge holder is needed to keep the processor firmly in position, and this is usually

Fig.3.20 *The polarising key*

supplied with the motherboard. However, in order to minimise the risk of damage in transit the cartridge holder is not normally supplied fitted to the board. There is more than one type of holder, but the most common type is in a single piece and is secured to the motherboard by four screws. There is also a two piece version of this arrangement, and versions of the single and two piece holders that are held in place by pins. The holder should be supplied with fitting instructions, but it is not too difficult to work out how it fits in place.

The Pentium II or III processor simply pushes down into the slot, and no more than moderate pressure should be needed to get it into place. As it moves down into position the clips on the cartridge holder will close and lock it in place. These must be set to the open position if it should be necessary to remove the processor again.

Heatsink

With the processor in place the heatsink and fan are then fitted. With socket 7 and 370 chips, fitting the heatsink and fan can be rather fiddly and in some cases you may find that the heatsink does not clip securely in place. The side-on view of Figure 3.21 shows the simple method of fixing that seems to be used for all Socket 7 and 370 heatsinks. Fitting the heatsink is just a matter of fitting one end of the spring clip on the heatsink under one of the plastic retaining clips on the socket. Without letting this end slip out of position, the other end of the clip is then secured on the other side of the socket. With some combinations of heatsink and processor it is a rather tight fit, but once the heatsink is actually in place it should stay there and work efficiently.

If the heatsink is a loose fit it may not work very well, and there is a real risk that before long it will become dislodged. If you look carefully at the clip that secures the heatsink to the motherboard you will probably find that part of the clip can be removed and repositioned further up the main section of the clip. Using this second position should result in the heatsink and fan being held in place much more securely.

With some processors, particularly the faster Socket 370 types, there may be a pad of a rather sticky rubber-like material on top of the processor. This is designed to ensure that there is a good thermal connection between the processor and the heatsink. Do not remove this pad and be careful not to damage it. Doing either of these could seriously reduce the efficiency of the heatsink, and could even result in the processor overheating.

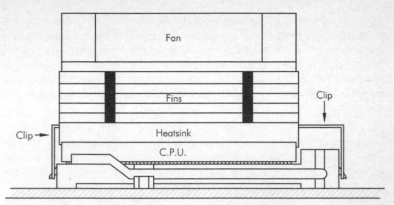

Fig.3.21 The heatsink and fan clip onto the ZIF socket

Slot 1 heatsinks seem to vary somewhat in the way that they are mounted on the processor. Usually it is just a matter of slackening off four screws, fitting the heatsink assembly in position, and then tightening the screws to clamp it in place. Apparently another type simply clips in place, but I have no first hand experience of these. Either way it might be a bit tricky to fit everything together, but the way in which everything fits together should be fairly obvious.

Fan

The cooling fan will require a 12-volt supply, and there are two normal ways of obtaining this. In the past the most common method was to obtain power from one of the 5.25-in. disc drive supply outputs of the power supply unit. There will not always be a spare output of this type, but the fan will almost certainly be

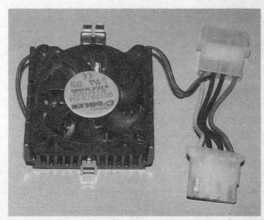

Fig.3.22 A cooling fan that takes its power from a 5.25-inch drive power cable

fitted with a lead that has two connectors (Figure 3.22). One of these connects to the output of the power supply and other connects to a 5.25-in. drive. This enables a single output of the power supply to provide power to both the cooling fan and one of the drives. If you use this method of powering the fan it is obviously not connected to the power supply until the motherboard has been finally installed in the case.

The alternative method, and by far the most common one these days, is to power the fan from the motherboard. Virtually all modern motherboards have a small three-pin connector that can supply 12 volts to the cooling fan, and most processor cooling fans are now fitted with this type of connector. There is no need to worry about getting this connector fitted the right way round, because it will only fit with the correct orientation. If the fan is powered in this way it should be connected to the motherboard as soon as it has been fitted on the processor. Modern motherboards often have more than one power supply output for a fan. If this should be the case the motherboard's instruction manual should indicate which output to use for the processor's fan, although it is not likely to matter too much if you use the wrong one.

Memory

The motherboard will either be designed to take memory as a mixture of SIMMs and DIMMs, or just DIMMs. Although SIMMs are not totally obsolete, they have been largely replaced by DIMMs (dual in-line memory modules). As memory in SIMM form now costs considerably more than an equivalent amount of DIMM memory, there is no point in buying SIMMs for a new PC. If you have some SIMMs you wish to use in the new PC they must be of a suitable type, which normally means 72-pin EDO SIMMs having a speed rating of 60ns. Slower SIMMs, or types containing another type of memory such as the fast page variety are unlikely to be usable. The old 30-pin SIMMs are not suitable for use with modern motherboards. Even if the motherboard will accept SIMMs, they may not be usable with all the processors that the board will accept, or some processors may have to be run at reduced speed. With the current low cost of DIMMs it is probably best to opt for these, but if you do use SIMMs read the "fine print" in the motherboard's instruction manual to ensure that they are fully compatible with the motherboard.

The DIMMs needed for most motherboards are the "PC66" type for a 66MHz bus, or "PC100" for a 100MHz bus. Most modern motherboards can use "PC100" DIMMs with a 66MHz bus frequency, but you should only try this if the instruction manual indicates that "PC100" modules

Fig.3.23 A DIMM ready to be pushed down into its holder

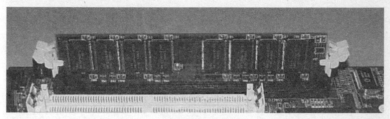

Fig.3.24 The DIMM pushed into the holder and locked in place

can be used in this way. New types of memory are coming along, and if you are building a "state of the art" PC it might be necessary to use "PC133" memory or some other new memory type. The instruction manual for the motherboard should explain which type or types of memory are usable.

Fitting memories

Fitting DIMMs is very easy, and it is impossible to fit them the wrong way round because the DIMM's circuit board has a polarising "key". This is just an off-centre notch cut in the circuit board that matches a bar in the DIMM socket (refer to Figure 2.15 in chapter 2). In fact there are two of these keys, and they are apparently in slightly different positions depending on the supply voltage of the module and the type of RAM fitted. This should make it impossible to fit a DIMM of the wrong type. Because one notch and bar are well off-centre it is easy to determine in which way around the module should go. The module simply drops into place vertically and as it is pressed down into position the plastic lever at each end of the socket should start to close up. Pressing both levers into a fully vertical position should securely lock the module in place, if the levers do not snap into this position anyway. Make sure the levers

Fig.3.25 A SIMM ready to be raised into the locking position

are pulled fully outwards before you try to fit the DIMM. Figures 3.23 and 3.24 respectively show a DIMM that is ready to be pushed down into place, and one that is locked in place. To remove a DIMM, simply press the two levers outwards as far as they will go. This should unlock the memory module so that it can be lifted free of the socket.

In my opinion at any rate, SIMMs are slightly more awkward to fit. Although in theory it is impossible to fit a 72-pin SIMM the wrong way round, in practice it does happen occasionally. This seems to be due to the rather flimsy and slightly too basic SIMM holders used on some motherboards. There is the usual polarising notch in the module and matching bar in the socket, but they are small and only very slightly off-centre. Also, there is one corner of the circuit board missing. The old 30 pin SIMMs were somewhat easier to deal with.

When fitting SIMMs, orient the motherboard so that the sides of the sockets having the metal clips, are facing towards you, and the plain sides are facing away from you. Take the first SIMM and fit it into the first socket, which is the one that is furthest away from you. The SIMM must be leaning toward you at about 45 degrees and not fully vertical (Figure 3.25). Once it is right down into the socket it should lock into place properly if it is raised to the vertical position (Figure 3.26). If it refuses to fit into position properly it is almost certainly the wrong way round. If you turn it through 180 degrees and try again it should fit into place correctly. You can then move on to the next socket, and fit the next SIMM in the same way. Note that SIMMs normally have to be used in pairs, but DIMMs can be used singly.

Fig.3.26 The SIMM raised to a vertical position and locked in place

Because SIMMs have to be inserted into their sockets at an angle, and the sockets are tightly grouped on the motherboard, you normally have to fit them in the right order. Otherwise you put in one SIMM which then blocks access to the socket for one of the others. You therefore have to work your way along the sockets in a methodical fashion. To remove a SIMM, pull the metal clips at each end of the socket outwards. The SIMM should then slump forwards at about 45 degrees, after which it is easily lifted clear of the holder. SIMMs have to be removed in the opposite order to the one in which they were fitted.

Drives

Once the memory modules have been fitted and the motherboard is installed in the case, the next step is to install the drives in the drive bays. There are plastic covers over the external drive bays, and these must be removed at the positions where drives are to be fitted. These are easily pushed out from the rear, but there will probably be a slight snag here in the form of a metal plate behind each plastic cover. These plates are partially cut from the case, and must be removed from any bays where externally accessible drives will be fitted. They can usually be left in place where other drives, such as the hard drive or drives, will be fitted. They are removed in the same way as other blanking plates in the case. Remove the plastic cover first. There are usually a couple of holes in the metal plate so that you can push out the plastic cover from the rear by poking a screwdriver through one of these holes. With a bit

Fig.3.27 The metal plate and plastic cover removed from a drive bay

of pushing and shoving it should be possible to turn the plate through about 30 degrees or so, although it can take a while to get the blanking plate completely free. You can then get hold of one edge, and with a bit of waggling the plate should soon break away from the case. With the plate and plastic cover removed (Figure 3.27) the bay is ready for the drive to be fitted.

It is likely that there will be more drive bays than drives, leaving some of the bays unused. It does not really matter too much which bays you leave unused, but where possible it is probably better to arrange things so that there is an unused bay between drives. Spacing out the drives often makes installation slightly less fiddly, and it can also make them easier to use.

With modern cases there should be no difficulty in fitting the drives since they slot direct into the bays. Suitable fixing screws should be supplied with the case, and will probably be included with some of the drives as well. It is best to only use the screws supplied with the drive or case, as they are suitably short. Screws even slightly longer might penetrate too far into the drive and cause severe damage. There are usually four mounting holes in each side of 5.25-inch drives, but it is only necessary to use two fixing screws in each side (Figure 3.28). Initially leave the screws slightly loose, and then manoeuvre the drive precisely into the right position so that its front panel is flush with the case's front panel. Then tighten the screws, being careful not shift the drive out of position.

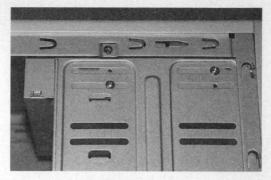

Fig.3.28 Two fixing screws per side will hold a drive in place

Depending on the design of the case you are using, it may or may not be possible to gain adequate access to both sides of the 3.5-inch drive bays. It necessary, remove the 3.5-inch bays from the case, fit the drives, and then replace the drive bays complete with the drives. With most cases, extricating the 3.5-inch bays only requires one or two screws to be removed, and then the bay can be slid away from the main casing. If this proves to be impossible it may be necessary to have the drives only secured to the bays on one side. This is not a desirable state of affairs, but it should hold the drives in place adequately. Some cases give better access to the underside of the 3.5-inch bays when the motherboard is not in the case, but you may then find it difficult to install the motherboard with the 3.5-inch drives fitted. You have to use your initiative when dealing with this type of thing, or you will simply end up going round in circles. Try to avoid the embarrassing mistake of fitting one or more of the externally accessible drives up side down.

Cabling

It is best to complete the cabling next, prior to installing the expansion cards (which tend to get in the way and make it difficult to fit the cables). The motherboard should be supplied complete with a basic set of connecting cables. For an ATX board this will probably just be a data cable for the floppy disc drive and and another one for the IDE drives. Both of these cables will support two drives, but in the case of the IDE drives you may prefer to buy a second cable so that the hard disc and the CD-ROM drive can be operated from separate IDE ports. In theory at any rate, this can give faster data transfers between the CD-ROM drive and the hard disc. If you settle for a single cable the drives can normally be connected to the IDE1 or the IDE2 interface, but the convention is to use the IDE1 port. Some motherboards will only boot from devices on IDE1, so this is the safe option.

If you are using a Ultra DMA66 interface and drive you will need the special cable that supports Ultra DMA66 operation. A suitable cable may be supplied with the drive or motherboard, but it will probably be an optional extra. It is a matter of reading the "fine print" in the instruction manuals to ensure that you use the correct cable.

In theory the IDE connectors are polarised and can only be fitted the right way round. In practice some of the connectors, especially on motherboards, are rather basic and are not properly polarised. The

plugs on the motherboards and drives should each have a cutout in the plastic surround, and this should match up with a protrusion on each plug. Figure 3.29 shows an IDE socket (top) and a matching plug (bottom), and the polarising keys are clearly visible. Some manufacturers take a "belt and braces" approach, and there may also be a missing pin on the plug

Fig.3.29 IDE and floppy drive connectors are polarised

and a blocked hole in the socket. If you look carefully at Figure 3.29 you will see that the connectors have the missing pin and blocked hole.

If you find that it is possible to fit the connectors either way round it is still quite easy to determine the correct method of connection. Computer data cables are made from a ribbon-like cable, which, unsurprisingly, is actually called ribbon cable. This is grey in colour, but there is a red mark or pattern running along one edge of the cable. This is the lead that connects pin 1 on one connector to pin 1 on the other connector. The instruction manuals for the motherboard and drive should have diagrams that show the position of pin 1 on each connector. In fact pin 1 is usually marked on the actual components, although you will probably have to look carefully to find these markings. Make sure that the red lead always matches up with pin 1 on the drives and motherboard, and the drives will be connected correctly.

Drive configuration

The two devices on an IDE port are called the "master" and "slave" devices. It does not matter which drive you connect to which connector on the IDE cable. Jumpers on the device itself control the role of an IDE device. If there is only one device on an IDE port it is normally set up as the master, but the system should work just as well if it is set as the slave device. The hard disc drive used to boot the system is normally the master device on IDE1.

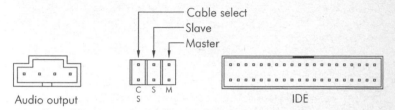

Fig.3.30 The configuration jumpers for a CD-ROM drive are buried in the connectors at the rear of the drive

The more or less standard arrangement for the jumpers on a CD-ROM drive is shown in Figure 3.30. The jumper is used to bridge the two "S" terminals if it is to be the slave device or the "M" terminals if it is to be the "master" drive. The "CS" (cable select) terminals and any others are not needed and are left unconnected, as are any other terminals in the block. Hard disc drives normally operate using a similar arrangement, but when used as a master device some drives are not quite as straightforward as this. A different jumper configuration can be needed depending on whether or not there is a slave device on that IDE port. You should always check the instruction manuals of IDE drives to see if there are any unusual aspects to the configuration, and then proceed accordingly.

Floppy drive

Connecting the floppy disc drive tends to cause a certain amount of confusion due to the unusual method of cabling used. The standard PC floppy disc drive cable consists of a length of 34-way ribbon cable, which is fitted with 34-way edge connectors and IDC connectors at the floppy drive end. 3.5-inch floppy drives require the IDC connectors, and 5.25-inch types connect to the edge connectors. The connector at the motherboard end is a 34-way IDC connector. Most cables are for twin drives, and therefore have two sets of drive connectors, which is some four in total. The maximum number of floppy drives that can be used is two and not four.

In a standard floppy drive set-up, the two connectors would be wired in exactly the same way. Pin 1 at the controller would connect to pin 1 of both drives, pin 2 would connect to both of the pin 2s, and so on. The two drives do not operate in unison, with both trying to operate as drive A, because there are jumper leads on the drives which are set to make one operate as drive A, and the other as drive B. These jumper blocks are normally a set of four pairs of terminals marked something like "DS0", "DS1", "DS2", and "DS3" (or possibly something like "DS1" to "DS4"). The instruction manual for the disc drive (in the unlikely event of you being able to obtain it) will make it clear which of the many jumper blocks are the ones for drive selection. Drive A has the jumper lead on "DS0", while drive B has it on "DS1".

Things could actually be set up in this fashion in a PC, but it is not the standard way of doing things. Instead, both drives are set as drive B by having the jumper lead placed on "DS1". The so-called "twist" in the cable between the two drive connectors then reverses some of the connections to one drive, making it operate as drive B. This may seem to be an unusual way of doing things, but there is apparently a good reason for it. If you obtain a PC disc drive, whether for use as drive A or B, the same drive configured in exactly the same way will do the job. This avoids the need for dealers to stock two different types of drive, which in reality is exactly the same type of drive with a slightly different configuration. In fact these days most drives sold for use in PCs do not have the jumper blocks, and are hard-wired to act as drive B.

The computer will still work if you get the connections to two floppy drives swapped over, but the one you required as drive A will be drive B, and vice versa. The connector at the end of the cable couples to drive A, while the other one connects to drive B. Figure 3.31 shows this general scheme of things. Getting the floppy drive cable connected to the new drive should be straightforward, because the two connectors should be polarised, so that they can not be fitted the wrong way round. The necessary "key" is just a small metal rod on the edge connector, which fits into a slot in the connector on the drive. There is the usual lump and a slot on IDC connectors, which serve the same function. If proper polarising is not implemented you will have to resort to checking for pin 1 and ensuring that the red lead on the cable carries this connection.

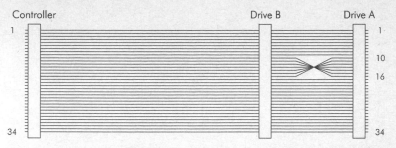

*Fig.3.31 Connection details for a floppy drive data cable. There may
be two different types of connector for each drive*

Termination resistors

Floppy disc drives used to be supplied with a block of removable
resistors, or resistors that could be switched out of circuit. The idea was
to have these termination resistors connected into circuit on the drive at
the end of the cable, but not on any drives along the way. Modern
floppy disc drives for use in PCs do not seem to have these resistors, or
if they do there is no way of cutting them out of circuit. Consequently
you will not have to bother with these resistors unless you are using an
old floppy drive in your new PC. The resistors should then be switched
out or removed if the drive is used as drive B (the one connected to the
middle of the cable).

Without an instruction manual for the disc drive it could be difficult to
deactivate the resistors. A search of the drive's circuit board will probably
bring to light a small component in a socket that can easily removed,
and this will probably be the termination resistors. Alternatively there
might be a switch or a jumper with markings that suggest it is for
deactivating the termination resistors. If not, the drive probably does
not have these resistors and it can then be used as is.

Ports

An AT motherboard does not have "proper" on-board connectors for
the serial and parallel ports. Instead, the basic connectors on the board
are wired to sockets mounted on the rear of the case, or in blanking
plates that are fitted behind any vacant expansion slots (see the section
that deals with expansion cards). The board should be supplied with
connectors and leads for the serial and parallel ports, and possibly

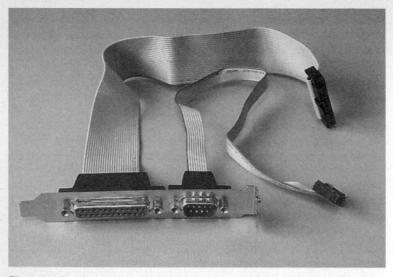

Fig.3.32 Parallel and serial port connectors fitted on a blanking plate

connectors and leads for the mouse port as well. Figure 3.32 shows a blanking plate fitted with connectors for one serial and one parallel port. These connectors are normally mounted in blanking plates, but it is usually quite easy to remove them from the plates and mount them on the case if preferred. Most PC cases have provision for a reasonable range of connectors on the rear panel. In the example shown in Figure 3.33 the parallel port is mounted on a blanking plate and the two serial ports (one 9-pin and one 25-pin type) are mounted on the case. However, the case does have provision for one parallel port and two 9-pin serial ports. The round connector is for the keyboard incidentally.

Fig.3.33 Some or all of the port connectors can be fitted on the case

If you wish to use a connector on the case instead of a

blanking plate it should be quite easy to make the transfer. At the ends of each connector there are two hexagonal threaded bushes, which accept the locking screws on the serial and parallel leads. These can be unscrewed with the aid of a pair of pliers, and the connectors should then readily pull free from the blanking plates. They can then be mounted on the rear of the case using the screws that have just been removed to bolt them back in place. Unless there is a shortage of vacant expansion slots I simply leave the connectors on the blanking plates. One potential problem with repositioning them on the case is that you might find that the "flying" leads attached to them would not reach to the connectors on the motherboard. Always check that the leads will be long enough before transferring a connector from a blanking plate to the case.

At the motherboard end of the cables the connectors are usually small IDC types, like the disc drive connectors. They should be polarised, but if not you will have to use the red lead to pin 1 method. Pin 1 might be indicated on the motherboard itself, but if not there should be a diagram in the instruction manual that shows pin 1 of every connector on the board. The serial and parallel port connectors are different sizes so it is impossible to get them swapped over.

Virtually all current AT motherboards have built-in USB ports, but the necessary leads and connectors to make use of them are normally an optional extra. The same is true of the IrDA port that can be used to provide communications with some digital cameras, portable computers, and other devices. Note that the IrDA port is not normally included in the cluster of on-board connectors of ATX boards. The connector and lead is usually an optional extra. If you wish to use these facilities you must be sure to obtain the correct lead and connector set, because there are minor differences from one manufacturer to another. In some cases the connectors at the motherboard end are different, in others they are the same but wired differently. Buy leads that are specifically designed for use with the particular motherboard you are using, and connect them in accordance with the instructions in the motherboard's instruction manual.

Power supply

Connecting an ATX power supply to the motherboard should present no major difficulties since there is just one connector and it will only fit the right way round. Some of these connectors can be reluctant to fit into place, but with firm pressure it should do so. An AT power supply has two leads that connect to the motherboard. The connectors are

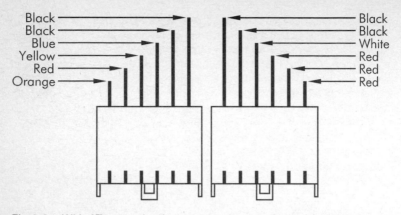

Black
Black
Blue
Yellow
Red
Orange

Black
Black
White
Red
Red
Red

Fig.3.34 With AT power leads connected correctly the black leads are grouped together in the middle

polarised, but there is nothing to stop you from getting them swapped over. The convention is for the black leads to be grouped together in the middle, as in Figure 3.34, and not at the ends of the row of connections. This type of power connector is a bit fiddly, and you need to be careful not to get everything shifted along by one connection point.

There should be more than ample power leads for the disc drives. The larger connectors are the ones for the 5.25-inch drives and 3.5-inch hard drives. Getting this type of connector into place can require a substantial amount of force. It can require even more effort to remove one again, so be prepared to use brute force with this type of connector. It is impossible to fit these connectors the wrong way round. The smaller connectors for the 3.5-inch drives are also polarised, and it should need relatively little force to connect them to the drives. If you find it difficult to fit these plugs into the drives you either have them upside down or out of alignment with the connectors in the drive.

Fig.3.35 A typical connector block

Connector block

The motherboard will have a connector block that accepts leads from various items on the case (Figure 3.35). This block is a common cause of confusion for newcomers to PC building because the facilities of the case

never seem to perfectly match up
with those of the motherboard. A
typical set of connectors for an
ATX case is shown in Figure 3.36.
There may be some features of
the case that are not supported
by the motherboard, and there
will almost certainly be several
motherboard features that the
case is unable to accommodate.
This is something where you

*Fig.3.36 A set of ATX case
connectors*

have to take a down to earth attitude, and provided a few basic features
are implemented on both,, which they will be, that is all that is needed to
get your new PC operating successfully. These are the functions that
you should be able to implement:

Power LED

This connects to what is usually a green LED on the front of the case
that switches on whenever the computer is operating. Note that an
LED, unlike an ordinary light bulb, will only work if it is connected with
the right polarity. The instruction manual for the motherboard will have
a diagram showing the functions of the various pins in the block, and
this with have a "+" sign on one of the pins that connects to the power
LED. The connectors on the leads that connect to the LEDs, etc., will be
marked with their functions, and the connector for the power LED might
have its polarity marked. If not, it is usually the white lead that is the
"–" connection and the coloured lead that is the "+" one. There is little
risk of a LED being damaged if it is connected with the wrong polarity,
so you can use trial and error if necessary.

IDE activity LED

This is sometimes called the hard disc light, and in days gone by it
would probably only switch on when the hard disc was active. However,
this light actually switches on when any IDE device is active, which these
days may include other IDE devices such as CD-ROM drives and CD
writers. This LED must be connected with the right polarity.

Reset switch

This is the switch on the front panel that can be used to reset the computer
if it hangs up. Its lead can be connected either way round. Some users
prefer not to connect this switch, so that it is not possible to accidentally

reset the computer. However, without the reset switch the only means of providing a hardware reset is to switch the computer off, wait at least a couple of seconds, and then switch on again.

Loudspeaker

This is the lead for the computer's internal loudspeaker, which is little used in modern computers. This loudspeaker is normally used to produce one or two beeps at start-up to indicate that all is well or a different set of beeps if there is a fault. The leads on this connector will probably be red and black, but it can actually be connected either way round and it is not polarised.

Power switch

This facility is not used with an AT power supply, which is switched on and off by way of an ordinary mains power switch. With an ATX power supply the on/off switching is controlled via a signal from the motherboard. The on/off switch connects to the power supply via the motherboard and the supply's main power output lead. Pressing the power switch turns on the computer, pressing it again switches off the computer, and so on. This switch appears to operate like a normal power switch, but note that the computer will be in the off state if the mains supply is removed and then reinstated. This lead can be connected either way round.

These are some of the functions that might be implemented on the motherboard, but they are non-essential:

Keylock

It used to be standard practice for PCs to have a key that could be used to operate a special type of switch fitted on the front panel. This switch enabled the keyboard to be switched off, thus preventing anyone from tampering with the PC while you were not looking. This feature was never very popular, and when control of PCs was partially handed over to the mouse it failed to fulfil its intended task anyway. It is probably not worth implementing even if this feature is supported by the case.

Temperature warning

Because modern PCs contain a lot of components that get quite hot it is now very common for some sort of temperature monitoring and warning feature to be included on motherboards. Exactly what happens when something in the PC starts to get too hot varies from one motherboard to another, but the internal loudspeaker will probably start to "beep", a warning LED might start flashing, or the PC might even switch itself off. If there is an output for a temperature warning LED and the case has a spare LED indicator, I would recommend implementing this feature. Note that the LED will only work if it is connected the right way round, and that it is normally switched on under standby conditions.

Suspend switch

This switch can be used to enable and disable the power management function. This is probably something you can live without, which is just as well since few cases have the necessary switch. There is sometimes an output for a LED which operates in conjunction with this feature.

There may well be other functions available, and it is a matter of consulting the motherboard's instruction manual for details of any additional features. However, unless the case has some spare switches and (or) LEDs any "extras" will only be of academic interest.

On the cards

By this stage the PC is nearly complete, and the only major task remaining is to fit the various expansion cards. Before the cards can be fitted it is necessary to remove the blanking plates in the rear of the case for the particular slots you will be using. Cases used to be supplied with blanking plates that were held in place by screws, but only a few up-market cases still use this method. The more usual method is for the blanking plates to be partially cut out. Those that are not required are simply broken away from the main case. The expansion cards should fit into place without having to push too hard. If a moderate amount of force fails to get one or more of the cards into position it is likely that the motherboard is slightly out of alignment with the case. Try slackening off the motherboard's mounting screws, fitting a couple of expansion cards, and then tightening the mounting screws again. It should then be easy to fit any remaining expansion cards, remembering to bolt the metal bracket of each card to the rear of the case (Figure 3.37).

If it is still difficult to fit one or two of the expansion cards the most likely cause of the problem is the metal bracket at the rear of the offending card or cards. If you look at the rear of the case you will notice that there are receptacles to take the bottom sections of the mounting brackets (Figure 3.38). With some expansion cards it is necessary to carefully

Fig.3.37 The expansion cards are bolted to the rear of the case

bend the lower section of the mounting bracket backwards so that it engages with the receptacle in the case. Everything should then slot nicely into position.

Finally

These days most CD-ROM drives are supplied complete with an audio cable that can connect the audio output at the rear of the drive to the audio input of the sound card. This enables audio CDs in the CD-ROM drive to play through the computer's speakers. This lead is not needed if you will only play audio CDs through headphones connected direct to the CD-ROM drive, or if you are not interested in playing audio CDs at all. On the other hand, you may as well fit it anyway just in case you need to use this facility at some future time. The connector at the sound card end of the cable will almost certainly be a type that is compatible with SoundBlaster cards. Most other sound cards now use the same type of connector, or have two audio input connectors including one SoundBlaster compatible type. There is still a slight risk that the cable

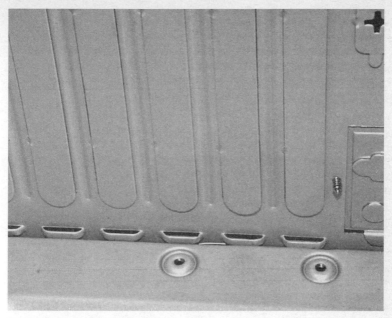

*Fig.3.38 The brackets on the expansion cards should fit into the
holders In the rear of the case*

will not be compatible with your sound card, and you will then have to
seek out a cable of the correct type.

You then have what is basically a complete PC base unit. There may be
one or two other leads that need to be connected, such as cables from
the soundcard or modem to the motherboard, but this is dependent on
both items of equipment supporting some extra features, and you wishing
to implement them. Where necessary, add any extra cables in
accordance with the instructions in manuals for the items of equipment
concerned.

One slight problem with the finished PC is that the interior tends to
become a tangled mess of cables (Figure 3.39). This problem is worse
with PCs based on an AT motherboard due to the extra cables to the off-
board port connectors. There are various products available from
electronic component retailers that help to tie cables together and to fix
them to the case. Tidying things up a little will not make the PC work
any better, but it can certainly aid reliability. Cables that are held in

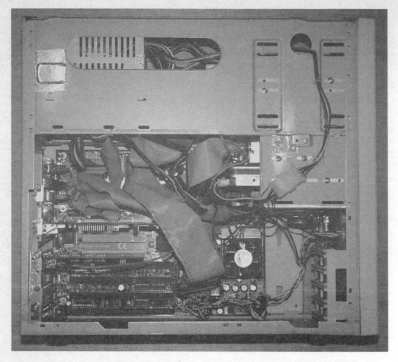

Fig.3.39　It is a good idea to tie down some of the cables in the finished PC

place properly are much less likely to work loose. They are also less likely to get mangled in one of the cooling fans! If you transport a PC that does not have the cables properly secured you should expect one or two of them to have worked loose by the time the PC arrives at its destination.

Testing

With the minor cabling completed the base unit of the computer is finished. Before connecting the mouse, keyboard, and monitor it is definitely a good idea to thoroughly check everything, making sure that all the cables are connected correctly and that none have been accidentally dislodged when working on the unit. None of the connectors lock into place, and it is very easy to dislodge one connector while fitting another. It is not possible to boot from the hard disc until it has been properly prepared, so initially try booting from something like an MS/DOS boot disc. Better still, use a Windows 98 start-up disc as this can provide CD-ROM support, and it will enable you to check that the CD-ROM drive is working properly.

When the computer is switched on it should go through the normal BIOS start-up routine. By default it will probably be set to auto-detect the IDE devices, and it will probably list the drives that are detected. If nothing happens, or there is any sign of a malfunction, switch off at once and recheck the entire wiring, etc. Assuming all is well, let the computer go through its boot-up routine so that you can check that it is more or less working correctly. If it is, the next step is to go into the ROM BIOS Setup program and configure the CMOS memory correctly. This is covered in the next chapter. Tips on getting troublesome PCs sorted out are provided in chapter 5.

Overclocking

Overclocking is sometimes referred to as the "free upgrade", and it is the practice of using electronic components beyond their maximum speed rating. It was sometimes used with motherboards that had 75MHz and 83MHz system frequencies, but chipsets that were only rated to operate at a maximum frequency of 66MHz. The motherboard's instruction manual usually contained one or two disclaimers, saying something along the lines that the board has the ability to use overclocking, but the manufacturer does not condone this practice. This may seem rather two-faced, but the manufacturer is basically saying that the board has the overclocking facility, but you use it at your own risk. Overclocking the motherboard's chipset is unlikely to damage anything, but good reliability can not be guaranteed. Since most modern chipsets can be used up to at least 100MHz this form of overclocking is now very uncommon.

These days overclocking is more usually in the form of the user trying to operate the processor beyond its normal clock frequency, and in some cases well beyond its normal clock rate. With some processors it often works quite well, but with most there is little or no scope for increasing the clock frequency. The Celeron is the favourite chip for overclocking, but only the slower versions having the 128k of on-chip cache are well suited to this treatment. Chips having ratings of 300 to 366MHz mostly work quite well with clock frequencies of up to 450MHz or so. The Socket 370 Celerons set the clock multiplier at the appropriate figure, and it is not possible to overclock them by increasing the multiplier value. With a suitable motherboard it is possible to overclock them by increasing the bus frequency from 66MHz to 75, 83, or 100MHz.

As an experiment I tried overclocking a 366MHz Celeron at 412MHz (75MHz x 5.5) and 456MHz (83MHz x 5.5) and in both cases no reliability problems were apparent. A clock frequency of 550MHz was totally unsuccessful though. In most cases an increase in the clock rate of more than about 10 percent is likely to result in failure, and a speed boost of around 10 percent or less will be barely noticeable. Also bear in mind that running a processor beyond its rated clock frequency results in an increase in power consumption and heat generation. This could result in the processor overheating and being destroyed. If you should damage a processor by overclocking it, or if it should fail for any reason while it is not being used within its normal operating parameters, it will almost certainly not be covered by the guarantee. If you experiment with overclocking techniques you do so entirely at your own risk. New PC builders would be well advised to do everything "by the book", and not risk problems trying to stretch any item of hardware beyond its normal limits.

Points to remember

Try to get a mental picture of how everything fits together before you actually start assembling the PC. Also make sure that you have everything you need including small items such as bolts and stand-offs.

Although most people only refer to instruction manuals as a last resort, this is not an option with the manual for the motherboard. Read it through carefully so that you can determine what configuration is needed for the particular processor you are using. It should also explain any special features that the board supports.

Do not rush construction of the PC. Proceed carefully, double-checking everything as you go, and the completed PC should work first time.

Unless the case limits access and makes it impossible, fit the processor, the processor heatsink and fan, and the memory modules before fitting the motherboard in the case. Any configuration switches or jumpers should always be set up before fitting the motherboard in the case. Working on the motherboard is much easier before it is fitted in the case, because it is much more accessible. Fitting the motherboard is often easier if the 3.5-inch drive bay assembly is removed from the case first.

The motherboard must be mounted on stand-offs so that the connections on the underside of the board are held well clear of the case. Otherwise short-circuits will occur and the motherboard could be damaged. There will probably be more mounting points on the case than the motherboard can handle, but there should still be sufficient mounting holes in the board to enable it to be properly supported over its entire area.

It is usually easier to mount the 3.5-inch drives if the drive bay is removed, the drives are fitted in the bay and then the whole drive and bay assembly is fitted in the case. Two mounting bolts per side are sufficient to securely fix the drives in place.

Most of the cables are properly polarised and will only fit the right way round. If one of the data cables is not properly polarised, refer to the instruction manuals to find pin 1 of the connector on the motherboard and the connector on the drive. The red lead of the data cable carries the pin 1 to pin 1 connection. The end of the cable having the "twist" connects to the floppy disc drive, and the other end connects to the motherboard.

The functions provided on the motherboard's connector block will probably not match up exactly with the functions supported by the case. The reset switch, IDE activity LED, and power LED are the only ones that are really needed. With an ATX case and power supply the on/off switch must also be connected to the motherboard. An AT power supply and case have a conventional on/off switch in the mains supply. Note that the front panel LEDs will only operate if they are connected the right way around.

To complete the PC fit the expansion cards, followed by any cables that connect to these cards. There will usually be an audio cable to connect the CD-ROM drive to the soundcard, but in most cases no other cables will be needed.

Have a final and thorough check of the completed PC before it is switched on and tested. Check that you have not accidentally dislodged one lead while fitting another.

The BIOS

Essentials

Before you can go on to install the operating system and applications it is essential to set up the BIOS correctly. A modern BIOS Setup program enables dozens of parameters to be controlled, many of which are highly technical. This tends to make the BIOS intimidating for those who are new to PC building, and even those who have some experience of PC construction. However, it is not necessary to go through the BIOS setting dozens of parameters in order to get the PC to perform satisfactorily. The BIOS should be customised to suit the particular motherboard it is fitted to, and it should set sensible defaults. In order to get the PC running well it is usually necessary to do nothing more than set a few basic parameters such as the time, date, and some drive details. Some "fine tuning" of a few other parameters might bring benefits, but is not essential. We will therefore start by considering the BIOS essentials before moving on to consider some of the other features that can be controlled via the BIOS. A detailed description of all the BIOS features would require a large book in itself, so here we will concentrate on those that are of most importance.

BIOS basics

Before looking at the BIOS Setup program, it would perhaps be as well to consider the function of the BIOS. BIOS is a acronym and it stands for basic input/output system. Its basic function is to help the operating system handle the input and output devices, such as the drives, and ports, and also the memory circuits. It is a program that is stored in a ROM on the motherboard. These days the chip is usually quite small and sports a holographic label to prove that it is the genuine article (Figure 4.1). The old style ROM is a standard ROM chip, as in Figure 4.2. Either way its function is the same. Because the BIOS program is in a ROM on the motherboard it can be run immediately at start-up without the need for any form of booting process.

Fig.4.1 The BIOS is a program stored in a ROM chip

The BIOS can provide software routines that help the operating system to utilize the hardware effectively, and it can also store information about the hardware for use by the operating system, and possibly other software. It is this second role that makes it necessary to have the Setup program. The BIOS can actually detect much of the system hardware and store the relevant technical information in memory. However, some parameters have to be set

Fig.4.2 An older style BIOS ROM chip

manually, such as the time and date, and the user may wish to override some of the default settings. The Setup program enables the user to control the settings that the BIOS stores away in its memory. A battery powers this memory when the PC is switched off, so its contents are available each time the PC is turned on. Once you have set the correct parameters you will probably not need to deal with the BIOS Setup program again unless you do some drastic upgrading.

Entry

In the past there have been several common means of getting into the BIOS Setup program, but with the motherboards available to amateur builders at present there is only one method in common use. This is to press the Delete key at the appropriate point during the initial testing phase just after switch-on. The BIOS will display a message, usually in the bottom left-hand corner of the screen, telling you to press the "Del" key to enter the Setup program. The instruction manual should provide details if the motherboard you are using has a different method of entering the Setup program.

The manual should also have a section dealing with the BIOS. It is worth looking through this section to determine which features can be controlled via the BIOS. Unfortunately, most motherboard instruction manuals assume the user is familiar with all the BIOS features, and there will be few detailed explanations. In fact there will probably just be a list of the available options and no real explanations at all. However, a quick read through this section of the manual will give you a good idea of what the BIOS is all about. A surprisingly large number of PC users who are quite expert in other aspects of PC operation have no real idea what the BIOS and the BIOS Setup program actually do. If you fall into this category the section of the manual that deals with the BIOS should definitely be given at least a quick read through.

There are several BIOS manufacturers and their BIOS Setup programs each work in a slightly different fashion. The Award BIOS and AMI BIOS are probably the most common ones fitted to the motherboards available to the do-it-yourself builder. The AMI BIOS has a Setup program that will detect any reasonably standard mouse connected to the PC, and offers a simple form of WIMP environment (Figure 4.3). It can still be controlled via the keyboard if preferred, or if the BIOS does not operate with the mouse you are using. The Award BIOS is probably the most common (refer to Figure 1.11 in chapter 1), and as far as I am aware it only uses keyboard control.

Fig.4.3 The AMI BIOS has a form of WIMP environment

Apart from variations in the BIOS due to different manufacturers, the
BIOS will vary slightly from one motherboard to another. This is simply
due to the fact that features available on one motherboard may be absent
or different on another motherboard. Also, the world of PCs in general
is developing at an amazing rate, and this is reflected in frequent BIOS
updates. The description of the BIOS provided here has to be a
representative one, and the BIOS in your PC will inevitably be slightly
different. The important features should be present in any BIOS, and it
is only the more minor and obscure features that are likely to be different.
The motherboard's instruction manual should at the least give some
basic information on setting up and using any unusual features.

Standard CMOS

There are so many parameters that can be controlled via the BIOS Setup
program that they are normally divided into half a dozen or so groups.
The most important of these is the "Standard CMOS Setup" (Figure 4.4),
which is basically the same as the BIOS Setup in the original AT style
PCs. The first parameters in the list are the time and date. These can
usually be set via an operating system utility these days, but you may as

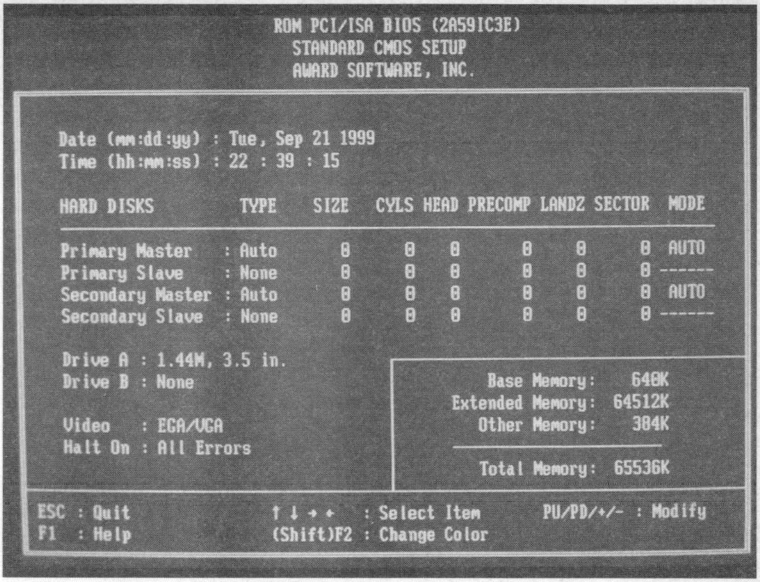

```
                    ROM PCI/ISA BIOS (2A59IC3E)
                       STANDARD CMOS SETUP
                       AWARD SOFTWARE, INC.

   Date (mm:dd:yy) : Tue, Sep 21 1999
   Time (hh:mm:ss) : 22 : 39 : 15

   HARD DISKS          TYPE    SIZE   CYLS HEAD PRECOMP LANDZ SECTOR  MODE

   Primary Master   : Auto      0       0    0      0      0     0   AUTO
   Primary Slave    : None      0       0    0      0      0     0   ------
   Secondary Master : Auto      0       0    0      0      0     0   AUTO
   Secondary Slave  : None      0       0    0      0      0     0   ------

   Drive A : 1.44M, 3.5 in.
   Drive B : None                              Base Memory:    640K
                                           Extended Memory:  64512K
   Video   : EGA/VGA                           Other Memory:    384K
   Halt On : All Errors
                                             Total Memory:   65536K

   ESC : Quit                ↑ ↓ → ←  : Select Item    PU/PD/+/- : Modify
   F1  : Help              (Shift)F2 : Change Color
```

Fig.4.4 An example of a standard CMOS Setup screen

well set them from the Setup program while you are in that section of the program. There are on-screen instructions that tell you how to alter and select options. One slight oddity to watch out for is that you often have to use the Page Up key to decrement values, and the Page Down key to increment them.

With virtually any modern BIOS a help screen can be brought up by pressing F1, and this will usually be context sensitive (Figure 4.5). In other words, if the cursor is in the section that deals with the hard drives, the help screen produced by pressing F1 will tell you about the hard disc parameters. It would be unreasonable to expect long explanations from a simple on-line help system, and a couple of brief and to the point sentences are all that will normally be provided.

Drive settings

The next section is used to set the operating parameters for the devices on the IDE ports. For the sake of this example we will assume that the hard disc is the master device on the primary IDE channel (IDE1), and

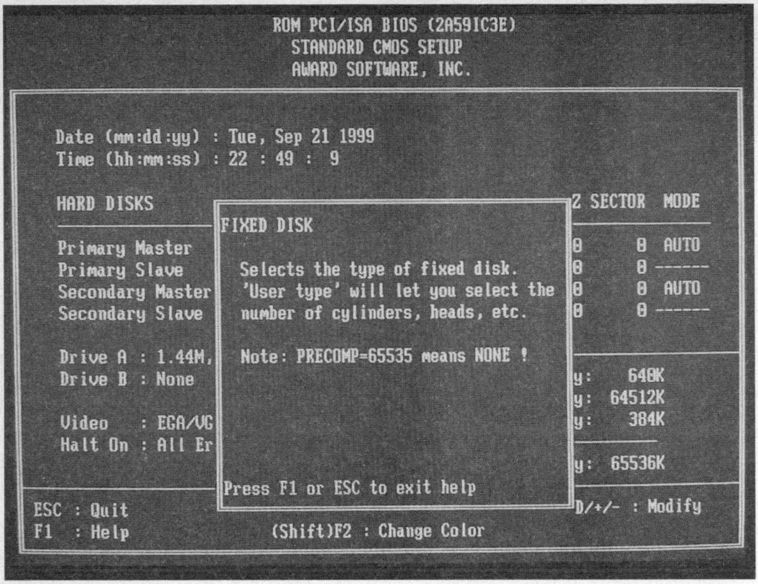

```
                    ROM PCI/ISA BIOS (2A59IC3E)
                      STANDARD CMOS SETUP
                      AWARD SOFTWARE, INC.

  Date (mm:dd:yy) : Tue, Sep 21 1999
  Time (hh:mm:ss) : 22 : 49 : 9

  HARD DISKS                                        Z SECTOR  MODE
  ───────────────┌─FIXED DISK──────────────────┐
  Primary Master │                              │ 0     0  AUTO
  Primary Slave  │  Selects the type of fixed disk. │ 0    0  ──────
  Secondary Master│ 'User type' will let you select the │ 0  0  AUTO
  Secondary Slave │ number of cylinders, heads, etc. │ 0     0  ──────

  Drive A : 1.44M,│ Note: PRECOMP=65535 means NONE ! │
  Drive B : None  │                              │
                  │                              │ y:    640K
  Video   : EGA/VG│                              │ y:  64512K
  Halt On : All Er│                              │ y:    384K
  ───────────────│                              │
                  │                              │ y:  65536K
                  └─Press F1 or ESC to exit help─┘
  ESC : Quit                                        D/+/- : Modify
  F1  : Help              (Shift)F2 : Change Color
```

Fig.4.5 Pressing F1 will usually bring up a brief help screen

that the CD-ROM is the master device on the secondary IDE channel (IDE2). If the manuals for the drives provide the correct figures to enter into the CMOS memory, and they certainly should do so in the case of hard disc drives, you can enter these figures against the appropriate device. In this case the hard disc drive is the "Primary Master". A modern AMI BIOS should have a setting specifically for a CD-ROM drive, and this can be used for the "Secondary Master" device. Simply setting everything at zero usually works where no CD-ROM setting is available. There are no primary or secondary slave drives, so simply enter "None" for these.

If you do not know the appropriate figures for your drives it does not really matter, because there is always an "Auto" option. If this is selected, the BIOS examines the hardware during the start-up routine and enters the correct figures automatically. This usually works very well, but with some drives it can take a while, which extends the boot-up time. There is an alternative method of automatic detection that avoids this delay. If you go back to the initial menu you will find a section called "IDE HDD Auto Detection" (Figure 4.6), and this offers a similar auto-detection facility. When this option is selected the Setup program examines the

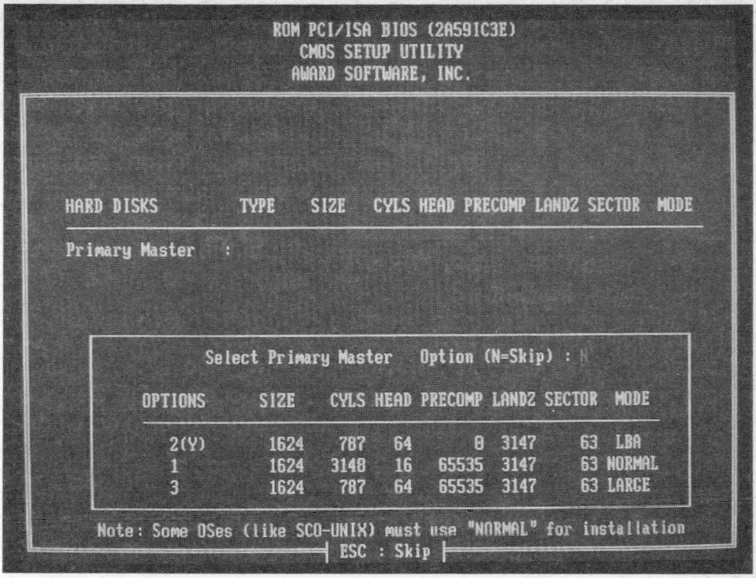

Fig.4.6 An IDE automatic detection screen in operation

hardware on each IDE channel, and offers suggested settings for each of the four possible IDE devices. If you accept the suggested settings for the hard disc drive (or drives) they will be entered into the CMOS RAM. There may actually be several alternatives offered per IDE device, but the default suggestion is almost invariably the correct one. After using this auto-detection facility it is a good idea to return to the "Standard CMOS Setup" page to check that the settings have been transferred correctly. Also, make sure that "None" is entered for the drive type where appropriate.

The last parameter for each IDE drive is usually something like Auto, Normal, LBA (large block addressing), and Large. Normal is for drives under 528MB, while LBA and Large are alternative modes for drives having a capacity of more than 528MB. Modern drives have capacities of well in excess of 528MB, and mostly require the LBA mode. The manual for the hard drive should give some guidance here, or you can simply select Auto and let the BIOS sort things out for itself.

Some users get confused because they think a hard drive that will be partitioned should have separate entries in the BIOS for each partition. This is not the case, and as far as the BIOS is concerned each physical hard disc is a single drive, and has just one entry in the CMOS RAM table. The partitioning of hard discs is handled by the operating system, and so is the assignment of drive letters. The BIOS is only concerned with the physical characteristics of the drives, and not how data will be arranged and stored on the discs.

Non-standard IDE

If you are using IDE devices other than hard discs and an ordinary CD-ROM drive it is advisable to consult the instruction manual for these drives to find the best way of handling their BIOS settings. CD-ROM writers and rewriters are normally entered into the BIOS as normal CD-ROM drives. A modern operating system such as Windows 98 should then recognise and install the drive, but only as a simple CD-ROM type. Some additional software, which is usually but not always supplied with the drive, will be needed in order to exploit its writing capabilities.

Other drives such as LS120 and Zip drives often have some specific support in the BIOS. It may even be possible to boot from these devices, although not necessarily with all operating systems. The instruction manuals for the drives should give detailed instructions on how to integrate them with any common BIOS.

Floppy drives

The next section in the "Standard CMOS Setup" is used to select the floppy disc drive type or types. All the normal types of floppy drive are supported, from the old 5.25-inch 360k drives to the rare 2.88M 3.5-inch type. You simply select the appropriate type for drives A and B. Select "None" for drive B if the computer has only one floppy drive. In days gone by you had to enter the amount of memory fitted, but with a modern BIOS the amount of memory is automatically detected and entered into the CMOS RAM. The "Standard CMOS Setup" screen will report the amount of memory fitted, and will display something like Figure 4.7.

Note that there is no way of altering the memory settings if they are wrong. If the BIOS reports the wrong amount of RAM there is a fault in the memory circuits, and the correct amount will be reported if the fault is rectified. Sometimes what appears to be an error is just the way the amount of memory is reported by the BIOS. For those who are new to computing the way in which the amount of memory is reported can seem rather strange. It should look very familiar to those who can remember the early days of IBM compatible PCs. The original PCs had relatively simple processors that could only address one megabyte of RAM, but only the lower 640k of the address range were actually used for RAM. The upper 384k of the address range was used for the BIOS ROM, video ROM, and that sort of thing.

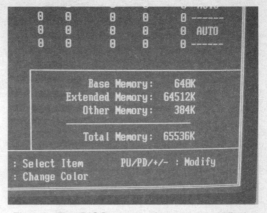

Fig.4.7 The BIOS reports the memory it finds. The user can not alter these settings

Modern PCs can address hundreds of megabytes of RAM, but the lowest one megabyte is still arranged in much the same way that it was in the original PCs. The BIOS therefore reports that there is 640k of normal (base) memory, so many kilobytes of RAM above the original one megabyte of RAM (extended memory), and 384k of other memory. This "other" memory is the RAM in the address space used by the BIOS, etc.

The final section of the standard set-up enables the type of video card to be specified, and the degree of error trapping to be selected. The BIOS will probably detect the video card and set the appropriate type, which for a modern PC will presumably be a EGA/VGA type. It is possible to select the old CGA and mono adapters, but these are obsolete and not used in modern PCs. The error trapping controls the way in which the computer responds to errors that are found during the BIOS self-testing routine at switch-on. The default of halt on all errors is probably the best choice, particularly when you are testing a new PC. Once the PC has been fully tested and is running properly you may prefer to alter this setting, but I would not bother.

Chipset

Setting up the standard CMOS parameters is probably all you will need to do in order to get the computer running properly, but it is a good idea to look at the options available in the other sections of the Setup program. The chipset Setup (Figure 4.8) controls things such as the port and

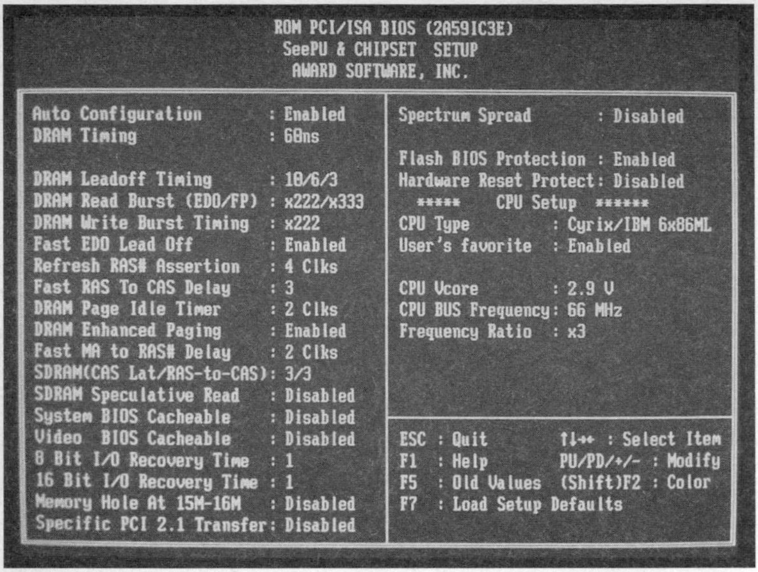

```
                    ROM PCI/ISA BIOS (2A59IC3E)
                     SeePU & CHIPSET  SETUP
                     AWARD SOFTWARE, INC.

 Auto Configuration    : Enabled   Spectrum Spread      : Disabled
 DRAM Timing           : 60ns
                                   Flash BIOS Protection : Enabled
 DRAM Leadoff Timing   : 10/6/3    Hardware Reset Protect: Disabled
 DRAM Read Burst (EDO/FP) : x222/x333  *****   CPU Setup  ******
 DRAM Write Burst Timing  : x222   CPU Type             : Cyrix/IBM 6x86ML
 Fast EDO Lead Off     : Enabled   User's favorite      : Enabled
 Refresh RAS# Assertion : 4 Clks
 Fast RAS To CAS Delay  : 3        CPU Vcore            : 2.9 V
 DRAM Page Idle Timer   : 2 Clks   CPU BUS Frequency: 66 MHz
 DRAM Enhanced Paging   : Enabled  Frequency Ratio   : x3
 Fast MA to RAS# Delay  : 2 Clks
 SDRAM(CAS Lat/RAS-to-CAS): 3/3
 SDRAM Speculative Read  : Disabled
 System BIOS Cacheable   : Disabled
 Video  BIOS Cacheable   : Disabled  ESC : Quit       ↑↓→← : Select Item
 8 Bit I/O Recovery Time : 1         F1  : Help       PU/PD/+/- : Modify
 16 Bit I/O Recovery Time : 1        F5  : Old Values  (Shift)F2 : Color
 Memory Hole At 15M-16M   : Disabled  F7  : Load Setup Defaults
 Specific PCI 2.1 Transfer: Disabled
```

Fig.4.8 This screen provides control over the chipset features

memory timing. You can "play" with these settings in an attempt to obtain improved performance, but higher speed may well produce lower reliability. Results should be quite good if you simply leave this section with the auto configuration enabled.

If you make a complete "dogs breakfast" of these settings it is possible that the PC could become unusable. This is not as drastic as it sounds because you can always go back into the BIOS and select the default settings from the initial screen. There will probably be an option to return to the "old" settings, which usually means the settings saved prior to the last time the BIOS Setup program was used. I suppose it is conceivable that changes made in the BIOS could render the computer unable to start up at all. I think that this is highly unlikely, but remember that the contents of the CMOS memory can always be wiped clean using the appropriate jumper on the motherboard. No matter how badly you scramble the BIOS settings it should always be possible to get back to the default settings and then "fine tune" things from there.

If you are using EDO memory you might find that there is a choice of 60ns or 70ns DRAM timing. This should obviously be set to the appropriate time for the memory modules you are using, but most modern motherboards only accept 60ns or modules, or do not accept EDO memory at all. If the PC is fitted with SDRAM it may be necessary to set the SDRAM CAS Latency. The default setting will probably be suitable, but check in the motherboard's manual to ensure that it is at the correct figure for the system clock frequency and SDRAM speed (10ns for PC100 or 12ns for PC66 modules) that you are using.

Cache

There are usually several cache options, covering the system BIOS, video BIOS, and the video RAM. The idea is to use fast memory, such as the level 2 cache, instead of the relatively slow BIOS or video RAM. Enabling these options will usually improve performance, but it is advisable to check with the video card's instruction manual that there are no likely compatibility problems.

Power management

Most operating systems and all modern motherboards seem to support some form of power management facility. In other words, the computer goes into some form of standby mode if there is no mouse or keyboard activity for a certain period. Most motherboards can also be switched to and from a standby mode via a peripheral such as a modem, and this also comes under the general heading of power management. A modern BIOS usually has a section dealing solely with power management (Figure 4.9). The Power Management Setup will probably be set to Disabled, and with some operating systems this is probably the best way to leave it. A lot of power management features can be controlled via the operating system these days, and you can sometimes get into a situation where the BIOS and the operating system are both trying to rule the power management roost. I normally disable this feature and only enable it if there is good reason to do so.

These days it is not uncommon for the motherboard to support more than one standby mode. The idea seems to be that the computer progressively shuts down the longer it is left unused. It will typically go from normal operation into the "doze" mode, followed by the "standby" and "suspend" modes. Operating the mouse or keyboard should always result in the computer returning directly to the "normal" mode, but it may take a few seconds to become fully operational if the motor of the hard disc has been switched off. Due to the high rotation speed of a hard disc it takes several seconds for it to reach its normal operating speed.

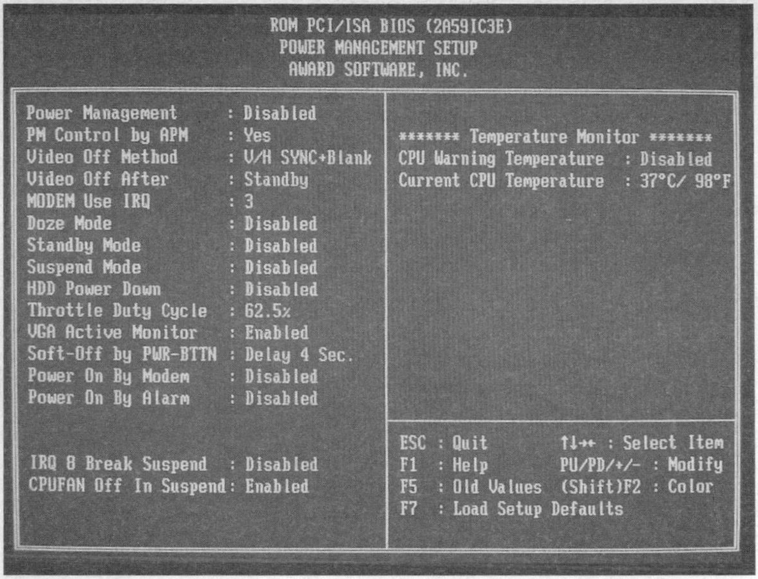

```
                    ROM PCI/ISA BIOS (2A59IC3E)
                       POWER MANAGEMENT SETUP
                        AWARD SOFTWARE, INC.

 Power Management     : Disabled
 PM Control by APM    : Yes          ******* Temperature Monitor *******
 Video Off Method     : V/H SYNC+Blank  CPU Warning Temperature  : Disabled
 Video Off After      : Standby       Current CPU Temperature  : 37°C/ 98°F
 MODEM Use IRQ        : 3
 Doze Mode            : Disabled
 Standby Mode         : Disabled
 Suspend Mode         : Disabled
 HDD Power Down       : Disabled
 Throttle Duty Cycle  : 62.5%
 VGA Active Monitor   : Enabled
 Soft-Off by PWR-BTTN : Delay 4 Sec.
 Power On By Modem    : Disabled
 Power On By Alarm    : Disabled
                                    ESC : Quit          ↑↓→← : Select Item
 IRQ 8 Break Suspend  : Disabled    F1  : Help          PU/PD/+/- : Modify
 CPUFAN Off In Suspend: Enabled     F5  : Old Values   (Shift)F2 : Color
                                    F7  : Load Setup Defaults
```

Fig.4.9 A typical screen for controlling power management features

The BIOS Setup program will probably permit adjustment of the delay times before each standby mode is entered, plus other details such as whether the processor fan is switched off when the "suspend" mode is entered. Of course, all this type of thing is only relevant if the power management feature is enabled. You may wish to "fine tune" the power management feature at a later time, but when initially setting up a PC it is probably best not to get deeply embroiled in this type of thing.

If the motherboard supports some form of external power management, and you wish to use this feature, it will have to be enabled in this section of the BIOS. Any feature of this type is always disabled by default. Any feature of this type will, of course, only operate if it is properly supported by the peripheral device or devices, and any extra cabling that it needed is properly installed.

CPU settings

Most motherboards now support at least a basic over-temperature detection circuit for the processor, and there are often various CPU

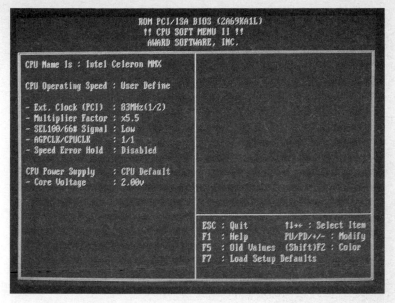

ROM PCI/ISA BIOS (2A69KA1L)
!! CPU SOFT MENU II !!
AWARD SOFTWARE, INC.

CPU Name Is : Intel Celeron MMX

CPU Operating Speed : User Define

- Ext. Clock (PCI)   : 83MHz(1/2)
- Multiplier Factor : x5.5
- SEL100/66# Signal : Low
- AGPCLK/CPUCLK   : 1/1
- Speed Error Hold   : Disabled

CPU Power Supply   : CPU Default
- Core Voltage   : 2.00v

ESC : Quit   ↑↓←→ : Select Item
F1 : Help   PU/PD/+/- : Modify
F5 : Old Values   (Shift)F2 : Color
F7 : Load Setup Defaults

Fig.4.10 An example of a separate screen for controlling CPU settings

threshold temperatures that can be selected. If the CPU goes above the selected temperature a warning is produced, and the PC usually shuts down as well. It is probably best to simply leave the threshold temperature at its default setting. You may find that the BIOS displays the current case temperature of the processor in this page of the Setup program. Anything below about 55 degrees Celsius should be completely safe.

If the motherboard is one that uses software control to set the correct parameters for the PC there could be a separate page for this (Figure 4.10), but it is often included in the chipset settings. The BIOS will automatically detect the processor type and should set the correct core voltage, bus frequency, and processor multiplier values. It is advisable to check that the BIOS has correctly identified the processor and set the correct values. It should be possible to set the correct figures manually if the BIOS makes a mistake, although it is very unlikely that it would do so. Otherwise, it should only be necessary to exercise manual control if overclocking is to be tried (see chapter 3).

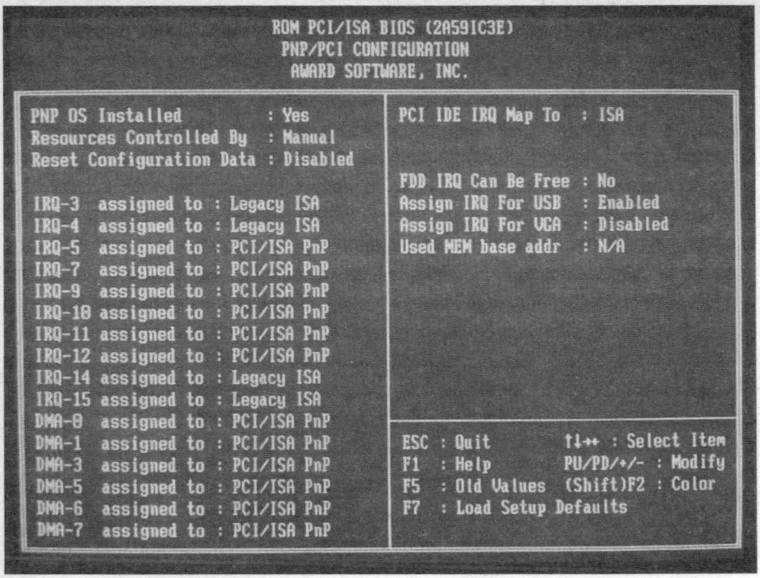

```
              ROM PCI/ISA BIOS (2A59IC3E)
                 PNP/PCI CONFIGURATION
                 AWARD SOFTWARE, INC.

 PNP OS Installed        : Yes      PCI IDE IRQ Map To  : ISA
 Resources Controlled By : Manual
 Reset Configuration Data : Disabled
                                    FDD IRQ Can Be Free : No
 IRQ-3  assigned to : Legacy ISA    Assign IRQ For USB  : Enabled
 IRQ-4  assigned to : Legacy ISA    Assign IRQ For VGA  : Disabled
 IRQ-5  assigned to : PCI/ISA PnP   Used MEM base addr  : N/A
 IRQ-7  assigned to : PCI/ISA PnP
 IRQ-9  assigned to : PCI/ISA PnP
 IRQ-10 assigned to : PCI/ISA PnP
 IRQ-11 assigned to : PCI/ISA PnP
 IRQ-12 assigned to : PCI/ISA PnP
 IRQ-14 assigned to : Legacy ISA
 IRQ-15 assigned to : Legacy ISA
 DMA-0  assigned to : PCI/ISA PnP
 DMA-1  assigned to : PCI/ISA PnP   ESC : Quit         ↑↓→← : Select Item
 DMA-3  assigned to : PCI/ISA PnP   F1  : Help         PU/PD/+/- : Modify
 DMA-5  assigned to : PCI/ISA PnP   F5  : Old Values   (Shift)F2 : Color
 DMA-6  assigned to : PCI/ISA PnP   F7  : Load Setup Defaults
 DMA-7  assigned to : PCI/ISA PnP
```

Fig.4.11 The PNP/PCI screen should be left untouched unless you know what you are doing

Note that any changes you make to the CPU settings may be ignored unless you activate an override setting. Also, when using a Socket 370 Celeron processor the motherboard will automatically set the correct multiplier value by reading information from the processor itself. It is not normally possible to set the multiplier manually even if the override setting is activated. The BIOS may seem to accept the new multiplier value, but when you exit the BIOS and reboot the computer it will operate with multiplier value set by the chip.

PNP/PCI

Unless you know what you are doing it is not a good idea to mess around with the PNP/PCI settings (Figure 4.11). The defaults should work perfectly well anyway. There will be the option of selecting "Yes" a PNP (Plug N Play) operating system is installed or "No" a non-PNP type is installed. Windows 95 and 98 are PNP operating systems, and the obvious setting is "Yes" if you will use either of these. In practice I have sometimes encountered problems if "Yes" is selected when using

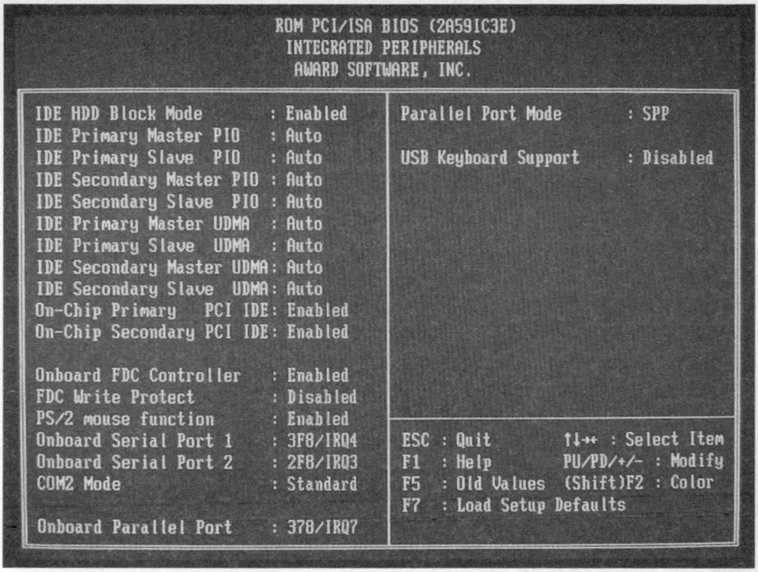

```
                    ROM PCI/ISA BIOS (2A59IC3E)
                      INTEGRATED PERIPHERALS
                      AWARD SOFTWARE, INC.

IDE HDD Block Mode        : Enabled    Parallel Port Mode      : SPP
IDE Primary Master PIO    : Auto
IDE Primary Slave  PIO    : Auto       USB Keyboard Support     : Disabled
IDE Secondary Master PIO  : Auto
IDE Secondary Slave  PIO  : Auto
IDE Primary Master UDMA   : Auto
IDE Primary Slave  UDMA   : Auto
IDE Secondary Master UDMA : Auto
IDE Secondary Slave  UDMA : Auto
On-Chip Primary   PCI IDE : Enabled
On-Chip Secondary PCI IDE : Enabled

Onboard FDC Controller    : Enabled
FDC Write Protect         : Disabled
PS/2 mouse function       : Enabled
Onboard Serial Port 1     : 3F8/IRQ4   ESC : Quit        ↑↓→← : Select Item
Onboard Serial Port 2     : 2F8/IRQ3   F1  : Help        PU/PD/+/- : Modify
COM2 Mode                 : Standard   F5  : Old Values  (Shift)F2 : Color
                                       F7  : Load Setup Defaults
Onboard Parallel Port     : 378/IRQ7
```

Fig.4.12 This screen provides control over the built-in ports

Windows 95. Consequently, I usually leave the default setting of "No" when using this operating system.

Integrated peripherals

The Integrated Peripherals section (Figure 4.12) provides some control over the on-board interfaces. In particular, it allows each port to be switched on or off, and in the case of the serial and parallel ports it also enables the port addresses and interrupt (IRQ) numbers to be altered. This can be useful when trying to avoid conflicts with hardware fitted in the expansion slots. There will be various parallel port modes available, but with a modern BIOS it is unlikely that there will be a Standard (output only) mode. The choices will probably be SPP, EPP, and ECP, which are all bi-directional modes. For most purposes either SPP or EPP will suffice. Only set ECP operation if you use the port with a device that definitely needs this mode.

If the motherboard supports infrared communications it may be possible to switch serial port two (COM2) between normal operation and infrared

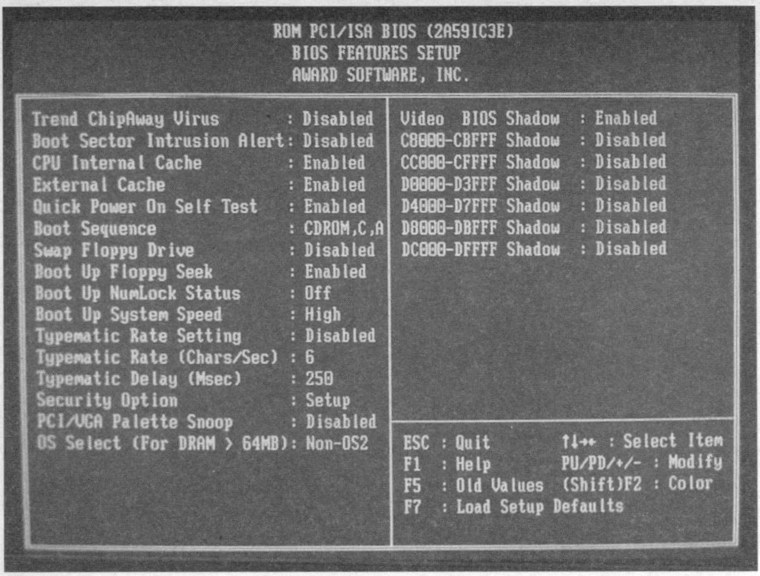

```
                    ROM PCI/ISA BIOS (2A59IC3E)
                    BIOS FEATURES SETUP
                    AWARD SOFTWARE, INC.

 Trend ChipAway Virus      : Disabled  Video  BIOS Shadow  : Enabled
 Boot Sector Intrusion Alert: Disabled  C8000-CBFFF Shadow  : Disabled
 CPU Internal Cache        : Enabled   CC000-CFFFF Shadow  : Disabled
 External Cache            : Enabled   D0000-D3FFF Shadow  : Disabled
 Quick Power On Self Test  : Enabled   D4000-D7FFF Shadow  : Disabled
 Boot Sequence             : CDROM,C,A D8000-DBFFF Shadow  : Disabled
 Swap Floppy Drive         : Disabled  DC000-DFFFF Shadow  : Disabled
 Boot Up Floppy Seek       : Enabled
 Boot Up NumLock Status    : Off
 Boot Up System Speed      : High
 Typematic Rate Setting    : Disabled
 Typematic Rate (Chars/Sec) : 6
 Typematic Delay (Msec)    : 250
 Security Option           : Setup
 PCI/VGA Palette Snoop     : Disabled
 OS Select (For DRAM > 64MB): Non-OS2  ESC : Quit        ↑↓→← : Select Item
                                        F1  : Help        PU/PD/+/- : Modify
                                        F5  : Old Values  (Shift)F2 : Color
                                        F7  : Load Setup Defaults
```

Fig.4.13 A screen for controlling the BIOS features

operation. When set to infrared operation it is possible for the PC to communicate with suitably equipped notebook computers and digital cameras that support infrared communications. However, the correct hardware add-on is needed on COM2 before this cordless communications will be possible. This dual role for serial port two seems to be less common these days and most motherboards now have entirely separate hardware to implement the IrDA facility. It is likely that the BIOS Setup program will give some control over the settings for this port, but simply accept the default settings. Only change the settings if this port is used with a piece of equipment that requires changes to be made. If any changes should be required, the instruction manual for the device concerned should explain exactly what needs to be altered.

BIOS features

The BIOS Features Setup (Figure 4.13) controls some useful features, but once again the default settings should suffice. The internal and external caches must be enabled if the computer is to operate at full speed. There are various boot sequence options, and eventually you might like to select C Only. In the mean time the boot sequence must include drive A, since this is the one that the computer must boot from until drive C is made bootable. The only exception to this is if you will be using an operating system that can be installed from a bootable CD-ROM. Any modern BIOS should have the option to use the CD-ROM drive as a boot drive, and this option must be selected if you intend to use this method of installation. Make sure that IDE HDD Block Mode is enabled, because the hard disc performance will be relatively poor if it is not.

After boot-up the NumLock key is normally on, but there is an option that switches it off after boot-up There are various BIOS address ranges listed, and the options of enabling or disabling shadowing of each one. By default the video BIOS will be shadowed, but the other address ranges will not. Shadowing of a BIOS is where it is copied into the computer's RAM and then run from there. The top 384k of the base memory is given over to the main BIOS, plus any other device that needs its own BIOS. In a modern PC this part of the memory map is occupied by RAM, but this RAM is normally disabled. When shadowing is enabled, the relevant block of RAM is activated, and the contents of the BIOS at that address range are copied into it. The point of this is that the RAM is faster than the ROM used for the BIOS, and using shadowing should speed up operation of the video card. Usually the only peripheral that has its own BIOS is the video card, but shadowing of other parts of the top 384k of memory can be enabled if necessary. If you have a peripheral device that will benefit from this treatment its manual should say so, and specify the address range that must be shadowed.

Floppyless

There are usually several options relating to the floppy disc drive or drives. One of these enables drives A and B to be swapped over. I am not sure why it would ever be necessary to have drive A operate as drive B and vice versa, but this facility is there if you should need it. Although at one time a floppy disc drive was an essential part of a PC, this is no longer the case. Other forms of removable disc are available, and with some operating systems it is now possible to install the system from a bootable CD-ROM. This removes the need to boot initially from a floppy disc. The problem with leaving out the floppy disc drive is that the BIOS will produce an error message each time that the computer is booted. There should be an option called something like "Floppy Seek", and by disabling this option the BIOS will not check for a floppy drive, and the error message will be suppressed. There may also be another option that has to be set when using Windows 95 without a floppy drive.

Other sections allow you to select a user password that must be entered before the PC will boot-up, load the default settings, save the new settings and exit, or exit without saving any changes to the settings. Being able to load the default settings is useful if you experiment a little too much and end up with totally unsuitable settings. It is worth noting that no settings are actually altered unless you select the "save and exit" option. If you accidentally change some settings and do not know how to restore the correct ones, simply exiting without saving the new settings will leave everything untouched. You can then enter the Setup program again and have another try.

Flash upgrade

If you look through the specifications for motherboards you will often encounter something like "flash upgradeable BIOS". In days gone by the only way of upgrading the BIOS was to buy a new chip, or pair of chips as it was in those days. Some of the ROMs used to store the BIOS were actually re-programmable, but only by removing them from the PC and putting them into a programmer unit. This was not a practical proposition for most users. New BIOS chips were very difficult to obtain, and you were usually stuck with the BIOS supplied with the motherboard.

The rate at which modern computing changes makes it beneficial to upgrade the BIOS from time to time in order to keep PCs up to date. For example, upgrading to a faster processor is sometimes only possible if the BIOS is upgraded first. With a modern BIOS there is no need to replace the BIOS ROM chip or to remove it from the motherboard for reprogramming. The ROM for a modern BIOS can be electronically erased and reprogrammed while it is still on the motherboard, and it is basically just a matter of running the appropriate program in order to upgrade the BIOS. The appropriate flash upgrade utility program should be supplied with the motherboard, and it should also be available for download from the manufacturer's web site. The manufacturer's web site is also the normal source for BIOS upgrades.

With a newly constructed PC it should not be necessary to upgrade the BIOS, and it is only possible to undertake the upgrade once the PC is to some extent "up and running". However, there can be problems with the BIOS and certain items of hardware and operating systems. If there is some odd problem with the finished PC it is a good idea to check the

FLASH MEMORY WRITER v5.35A
Copyright (C) 1996, Award Software, Inc.,

For i430TX-8679-2A59IC3EC   DATE : 05/29/98
   Flash Type - 28F010 /12V

File Name to Program : 5AGM2V3

Error Message : Do You Want To Save Bios (Y/N)

Fig.4.14 A typical flash memory writer program in operation

web site of the motherboard manufacturer to see if there is an upgrade
that will fix the problem.

Risks

The instruction manual for the motherboard should have a detailed
explanation of how to go about the upgrade, and there will probably be
a "read.me" file with the upgrade software that also gives this information.
The upgrade is usually in the form of two files, one of which is the program
that actually performs the upgrade for you. The other is the new data for
the ROM. It is only fair to point out that a BIOS upgrade of this type is a
bit risky. You need to be absolutely certain that the data file you are
using is the correct one for your motherboard. Using the wrong BIOS
data file could easily render the computer unusable, and if it will not
boot-up correctly it is impossible to restore the original BIOS.

Another slight worry is that a power failure during the upgrade could
leave the PC with a BI (half a BIOS)! With an incomplete or corrupted

BIOS it is unlikely that the PC could be rebooted to restore the original or complete the upgrade. It only takes a few seconds to carry out the upgrade, so you would be very unlucky indeed if a power failure interrupted the process, but it is a slight risk.

The upgrade program usually has to be run from MS/DOS, and is usually very simple to operate (Figure 4.14). After you have supplied the name of the data file for the new BIOS (including any extension to the filename) the program should give the option of saving the existing BIOS onto disc. It is as well to do this so that you can revert to the original BIOS if the new version proves to be troublesome. After you have confirmed that you wish to continue with the upgrade the new data will be written to the BIOS ROM chip. Do not touch the computer during the flash upgrade, just stand back and let the upgrade program get on with it. The computer is then ready for rebooting and checking to see if the new BIOS has the desired effect.

Points to remember

The BIOS helps the operating system to deal with the hardware, particularly the drives and memory. It stores masses of information about the hardware in CMOS RAM which retains its contents when the computer is switched off. These can be controlled via the Setup program built into the BIOS.

The normal way into the BIOS Setup program is by pressing the Del key during the initial start up routine. A message will appear on the screen at the appropriate time. If the BIOS you are using has a different method of entering the Setup program the motherboard's instruction manual should explain what to do.

It is essential to go into the BIOS to ensure that it is set up correctly. If you simply try to bypass this part of PC building it is unlikely that the PC will work really well, and it may well be impossible to get it working properly at all. Vital information required by the operating system may be missing.

Do not be intimidated by the BIOS Setup program. With a modern BIOS there are numerous parameters that can be adjusted, but to a large extent you can leave the BIOS to sort things out for itself.

As a minimum, set the time and date and check that the various drives (including any floppy drives) are properly installed. It is also advisable to check to see if there are any memory settings that might need adjustment.

The manual provided with hard disc drive should give the correct parameters to enter into the Setup program, but satisfactory results should be obtained if you simply opt for automatic detection.

If the BIOS detects the processor and sets the core voltage, bus frequency, and multiplier value, check that they are correct. Do not experiment with overclocking unless you know what you are doing and are prepared to foot the bill for any damage caused.

Read the section of the motherboard's manual that deals with the BIOS. Each BIOS is slightly different, and the only way to find out if the one you are using has some special features you should know about is to read through the manual.

It is worthwhile adjusting things such as the Numlock setting to suit your own preferences, so check through the available parameters for any that you can usefully customise.

You may need to alter the parallel port's operating mode if you use any advanced parallel port devices that require high speed data transfers.

Remember to save the new parameters before exiting the Setup program. Alternatively, if you have made a mess of things you can exit without saving the scrambled settings.

It is very unlikely that "playing" with the BIOS settings will cause any damage to the hardware, and if things get into a complete mess you can always return to the default settings. However, simply playing around with settings to see what happens is not really a good idea.

Do not experiment with the flash memory writing program. A careless error here could easily render the computer unusable, and the only solution might be a replacement motherboard. A BIOS upgrade is something you only undertake if you really need to, and it is then essential to proceed with great care.

Operating systems

Legalities

With the BIOS set up correctly it is time to install the operating system. It has to be pointed out that it is not acceptable to simply "borrow" an operating system from one computer and install it on another. You should have a licence for each copy of an operating system that is installed on your PCs. If you are scrapping an old PC then it is perfectly legitimate to use all the software from the old PC on the new one, since it will still be running on a single computer. If you are not scrapping an old PC it is necessary to buy an operating system for your newly constructed computer.

I think I am correct in stating that the full version of Windows 98, like Windows 95 that preceded it, is only sold with new PCs or with major items of hardware. If you have a qualifying upgrade product this does not matter, since you would presumably buy the upgrade version anyway. If not, you should still be able to buy the full product provided you purchase a major item of hardware at the same time. In this context a major item of hardware seems to mean either a motherboard or a hard disc drive. As far as I am aware, there is no restriction of this type with other operating systems such as Windows NT4 Workstation and BEOS. Of course, with a "free" operating system such as Linux you can install as many copies as you wish on as many PCs as you like. However, there may be some restrictions on the use of certain programs provided with the operating system, so it is as well to check the "fine print".

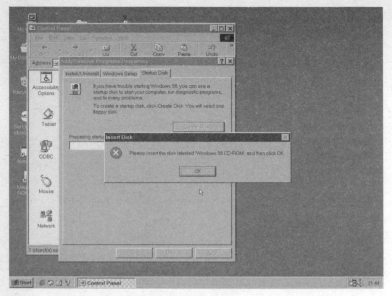

Fig.5.1 Creating a Windows 98 Startup disc

Formatting

The method used to install the operating system depends on which particular system you will be using, and there may be more than one way of handling things. With MS/DOS, Windows 3.1, Windows 95, and Windows 98 the hard disc drive must be formatted before the operating system can be installed. Start by rebooting the computer. With the computer booted-up and running MS-DOS or the Windows 95/98 equivalent of MS-DOS, the hard drive will not be accessible. Modern hard disc drives are supplied with the low level formatting already done, but they still require high-level formatting using the MS-DOS "FORMAT" program. However, you must first prepare the disc using the "FDISK " command.

The system disc used to boot the computer should contain copies of both FDISK and FORMAT, and it is also helpful if this disc contains a simple text editor program such as the MS-DOS EDIT program. With a Windows 98 set-up disc both of these programs will be placed on the disc for you when it is created. To create the disc from the Windows 98 desktop select Start, Settings, Control Panel, Add/Remove Programs,

Startup Disc, and finally Create Disc (Figure 5.1). Note that you will be asked for the Windows 98 CD-ROM, because some of the files required are not normally stored on the hard disc.

With an MS/DOS boot disc you must copy the programs onto the disc yourself, from an MS/DOS installation on a hard disc drive. It is better to use a Windows 98 disc rather than the Windows 95 equivalent or a "real" MS/DOS disc. Windows 98 provides better support for large hard disc drives. Using earlier versions of MS/DOS you may find that the disc is used inefficiently, and that the disc has to be organised as if it were actually several relatively small discs. The drive may be supplied with software that helps to work around these problems, but it is better to use a modern operating system that can handle large hard disc drives properly.

Large drives

FDISK is used to create one or more DOS partitions, and with discs of 2.1 gigabytes or less you may wish to have the whole of the disc as a single partition. The hard disc drive then becomes drive C. By creating further partitions it can also operate as drive D, drive E, etc. The primary partition is the boot disc, and this is where the operating system must be installed. The MS/DOS and Windows 95 file systems set the 2.1-gigabyte partition limit. There is also an 8.4-gigabyte limit on the physical size of the drive. With Windows 98 and any reasonably modern BIOS these limits do not apply, but you must use the FAT32 file system. To do this simply answer yes when FDISK is first run, and you are asked if you require support for large hard disc drives. Even if you do not wish to have a large disc organised as one large partition, it is still best to opt for large hard disc support. FAT32 utilizes the available disc space more efficiently and reduces wastage. Note that if you only require a single partition you must still use the FDISK program to set up this single partition, and that the FORMAT program will not work on the hard drive until FDISK has created a DOS partition.

Some hard discs are supplied complete with partitioning software that will also format the disc and add the system files, which will be copied from the boot disc. Where a utility program of this type is available it is probably better to use it instead of the FDISK and FORMAT programs. These MS-DOS programs are fairly straightforward in use, but using the software supplied with the drive will almost certainly be even easier. If you use the FDISK and FORMAT programs, make sure that you are using modern versions of them. Versions of MS/DOS earlier than version

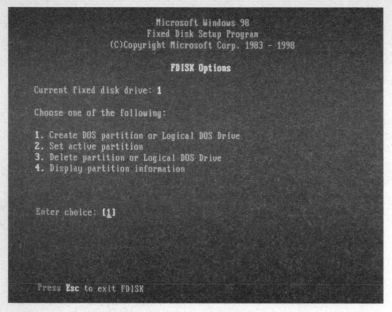

Microsoft Windows 98
Fixed Disk Setup Program
(C)Copyright Microsoft Corp. 1983 - 1998

FDISK Options

Current fixed disk drive: **1**

Choose one of the following:

1. Create DOS partition or Logical DOS Drive
2. Set active partition
3. Delete partition or Logical DOS Drive
4. Display partition information

Enter choice: [**1**]

Press **Esc** to exit FDISK

Fig.5.2 The main FDISK menu has four options

3.3 are not able to provide two partitions, and are not really suitable for use with a modern PC.

Using FDISK

Once you are in FDISK there is a menu offering these four choices (see also Figure 5.2):

1. Create DOS partition or logical DOS drive

2. Set the active partition

3. Delete partition or logical DOS drive

4. Display partition information

The first thing we need to do is create a DOS partition, so select option one, which will be the default. This takes you into a further menu offering these three options (Figure 5.3):

1. Create primary DOS partition

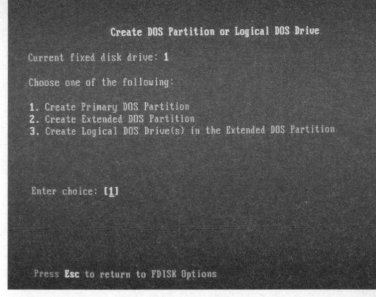

Create DOS Partition or Logical DOS Drive

Current fixed disk drive: **1**

Choose one of the following:

1. Create Primary DOS Partition
2. Create Extended DOS Partition
3. Create Logical DOS Drive(s) in the Extended DOS Partition

Enter choice: [**1**]

Press **Esc** to return to FDISK Options

Fig.5.3 The FDISK partition creation menu

2. Create extended DOS partition

3. Create logical DOS drive(s) in the extended DOS partition

It is a primary DOS partition that is required, so select option one, which should again be the default. You will then be asked if you wish to use the maximum space for the partition and make it the active partition. If you answer yes, the whole disc, or as much of it as FDISK can handle, will be used for the partition. It will also be made active, which simply means that this is the partition that the computer will try to boot from. This is the partition to which the operating system should be installed. If you answer no, you will then have to specify the size of the primary partition in megabytes. This creates the partition, but does not make it active. Having created the partition you the press the Escape key to return to the original menu. It is a good idea to select option four to check that the partition has been created successfully (Figure 5.4).

If you did not use the maximum space for the partition it will not have been made active. To do this select option two from the main menu and

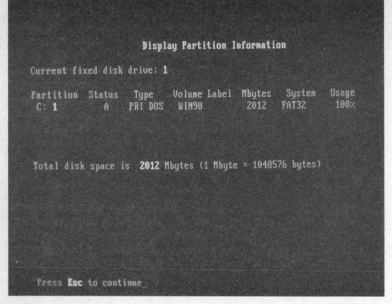

Fig.5.4 Using FDISK to check partition information

then enter the number of the partition you wish to make active. As there is only one partition this will obviously be partition number one. Press return to implement this command, and then press the Escape key to return to the main menu again. It is then a good idea to use option four once again to ensure that everything has gone smoothly. In the Status column there should be an "A" to indicate that partition one is active (as in Figure 5.4).

If a further partition is required select option one, and then option two, which is "Create extended DOS partition" (Figure 5.5). Enter the size of the partition you require and press the Return key to create the partition. Then press the Escape key, which will bring up a message saying "No logical drives defined" (Figure 5.6). In other words, you have created a partition, but as yet it does not have a drive letter. Assuming you require all the space in the partition to be one logical drive, simply press the Return key. This will make the partition drive D, and a screen giving this information will appear (Figure 5.7). Press the Escape key to return to the main menu, and use option four to check that the partition has been created successfully.

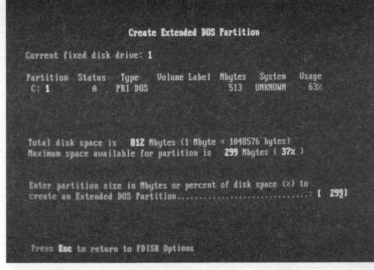

Fig.5.5 Creating an extended DOS partition

Formatting

Having created the partitions you require, the "FORMAT" command can then be run. First you will have to press the Escape key twice to exit FDISK, and then the computer must be rebooted so that the new partition information takes effect. To format drive C and place the system files onto it use this command:

format C: /s

This will bring up a warning to the effect that all data in drive C will be lost if you proceed with the format. As yet there is no data to lose, so answer yes to proceed with the formatting. It might take several minutes to complete the task, since there are a large number of tracks to be processed and checked. If the hard disc has more than one partition and is operating as drive C, drive D, etc., each partition must formatted using a separate "FORMAT" command. Of course, the system should only be placed on disc C, so for the other logical drives do not use the "/s" addition to the command. This would not actually prevent drive D from working, but it would waste disc space on system files that would never be used. To format drive D this command would be used:

format D:

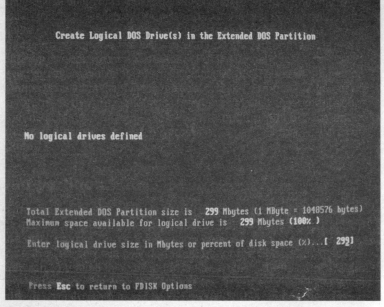

Create Logical DOS Drive(s) in the Extended DOS Partition

No logical drives defined

Total Extended DOS Partition size is   299 Mbytes (1 MByte = 1048576 bytes)
Maximum space available for logical drive is   299 Mbytes (100%)

Enter logical drive size in Mbytes or percent of disk space (%)...[299]

Press Esc to return to FDISK Options

*Fig.5.6 Creating an extra partition does not automatically create a
logical drive*

Windows

If you are still using MS-DOS, the PC is more or less ready to use once
the hard drive is bootable. You will have to install all your applications
software or course, and it is a good idea to copy the MS-DOS support
files to a directory call "DOS", or something similar. The later versions of
MS/DOS have an installation program that will do all this for you.
Windows 3.1 can be installed onto the hard disc in much the same way
as applications programs. For most users, putting the MS-DOS operating
system onto the hard disc is simply a stepping-stone to installing
Windows 95/98. In the unlikely event that you have the floppy disc version
of Windows 95/98 there should be no difficulty in loading it onto the
hard disc once the hard disc is bootable. You may find that you need to
install the mouse in MS-DOS first, but otherwise it can be installed onto
the bare drive.

The situation is similar with the CD-ROM version, but it is necessary to
install the mouse and the CD-ROM drive into MS-DOS before the
Windows Setup program can be run. This is simply because MS-DOS

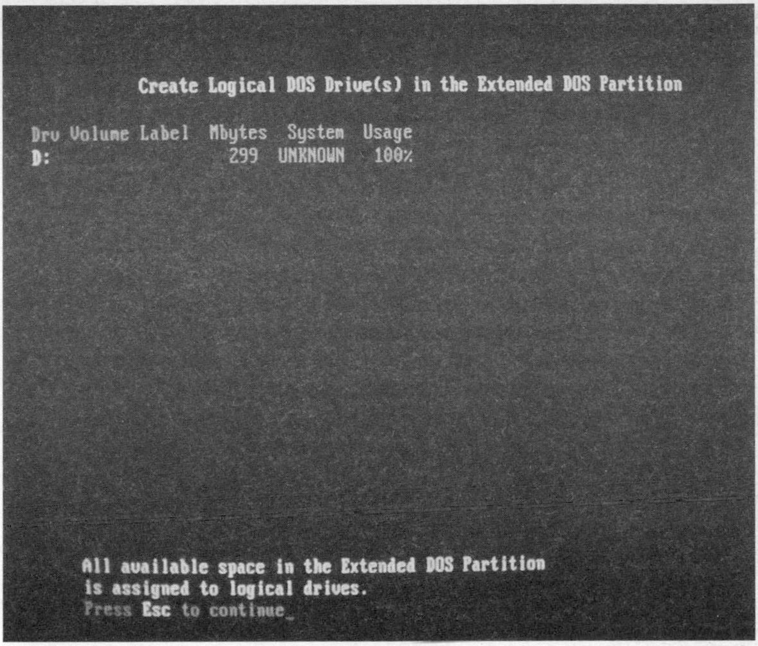

Fig.5.7 This screen confirms that logical drive D: has been created

will not automatically recognise the CD-ROM drive and designate it as drive D, or whatever. Just the opposite in fact, and MS-DOS will totally ignore the CD-ROM drive until the installation process has been completed and the computer has been rebooted.

The mouse and the CD-ROM drive should be supplied complete with installation software that largely does the installation for you. Some CD-ROM manufacturers supply the MS-DOS MSCDEX.EXE file, which is needed to integrate the CD-ROM drive with MS-DOS, but in most cases you will have to ensure that it is already on the hard disc. This file is supplied as part of MS-DOS 5 and 6, and should be placed on the hard disc if you install all the MS-DOS support files. It is installed into the C:\Windows\Command directory once Windows 95/98 is installed, but this is obviously of no use at this stage, as Windows is not yet installed on the PC. If necessary, "borrow" this file from another PC by copying it onto a floppy disc, and then copying it to the hard disc drive. Alternatively, if you have a Windows 98 "recovery disc", boot up from this and choose CD-ROM support when asked to select the start-up mode. This should

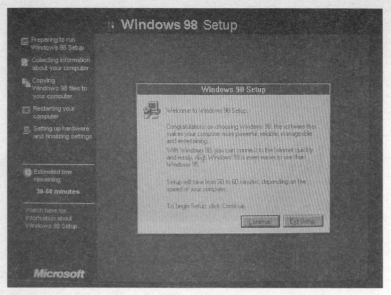

Fig.5.8 The initial screen of the Windows 98 Setup program

provide access to the CD-ROM drive so that the Windows installation disc can be run.

Windows Setup

Once the mouse and CD-ROM drive have been installed it should be possible to run the Setup program on the Windows 95/98 installation disc. The Scandisk utility will run first and will check for errors on the hard disc drives and logical drives. Assuming all is well, press the "x" key to exit Scandisk and go into the first screen of the Windows Setup program (Figure 5.8). It is then just a matter of following the on-screen prompts to complete the Windows installation. Note that you can install the upgrade version of Windows 95 or 98 onto a "clean" hard disc, and that it is not essential to load your old version of Windows first so that you have something to upgrade. However, during the installation process you will probably be asked to prove that you have a qualifying upgrade product by putting the Setup disc into the floppy drive or CD-ROM drive, as appropriate. Do not throw away or recycle your old Windows discs, as this could leave you unable to reinstall the Windows upgrade.

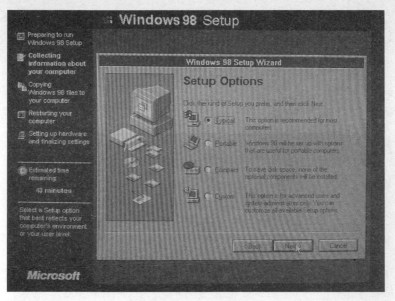

Fig.5.9 Four types of installation are offered by the Setup program

You will be asked to select the directory into which Windows will be installed, but unless there is good reason to do otherwise, simply accept the default (C:\Windows). You will be offered several installation options (Figure 5.9), but for most users the default option of a "Typical" installation will suffice. Remember that you can add and delete Windows components once the operating system is installed, so you are not tied to the typical installation forever. The "Custom" options enables the user to select precisely the required components, but this can be time consuming and you need to know what you are doing. The "Compact" option is useful if hard disc space is limited, but with a new PC the hard disc will presumably be large enough to make this option superfluous.

After providing language information, etc., the program will progress to the main installation screen (Figure 5.10), and from thereon installation is largely automatic. The computer will reboot itself two or three times during the installation process, so if you opted to produce a Windows 98 start-up disc during the initial set-up procedure remember to remove this from the floppy drive. Otherwise the computer might reboot from the floppy rather than the hard disc, which would interfere with the installation process. Eventually you should end up with a basic Windows 98 installation, and the familiar initial screen (Figure 5.11).

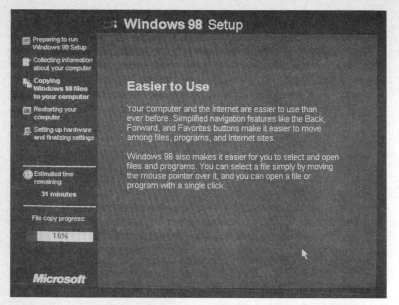

Windows 98 Setup

Preparing to run
Windows 98 Setup

Collecting information
about your computer

Copying
Windows 98 files
to your computer

Restarting your
computer

Setting up hardware
and finalizing settings

Estimated time
remaining:

31 minutes

File copy progress:

16%

Easier to Use

Your computer and the Internet are easier to use than
ever before. Simplified navigation features like the Back,
Forward, and Favorites buttons make it easier to move
among files, programs, and Internet sites.

Windows 98 also makes it easier for you to select and open
files and programs. You can select a file simply by moving
the mouse pointer over it, and you can open a file or
program with a single click.

Microsoft

Fig.5.10 *Once the main installation screen is reached installation
is largely automatic*

There will probably still be a certain amount of work to be done in order
to get all the hardware fully installed, the required screen resolution set,
and so on. To alter the screen resolution and colour depth, go to the
control panel and double-click on the Display icon. Then left-click on
the Settings tab to bring up a screen of the type shown in Figure 5.12. It
is then just a matter of using the on-screen controls to set the required
screen resolution and colour depth. To use the new settings left-click
the Apply button. It may be necessary to let the computer reboot in
order to use the new settings, but in most cases they can be applied
without doing this. Instead Windows will apply the new settings for a
few seconds so that you can see that all is well. Simply left-click on the
Yes button to start using the new settings.

If there is a problem with the picture stability, do nothing, and things
should return to the original settings after a few seconds. This should
not really happen if the monitor is installed correctly, because Windows
will not try to use scan rates that are beyond the capabilities of the installed
monitor. If a problem of this type should occur, check that the monitor is
installed properly. In the Display window of Control Panel select Settings,

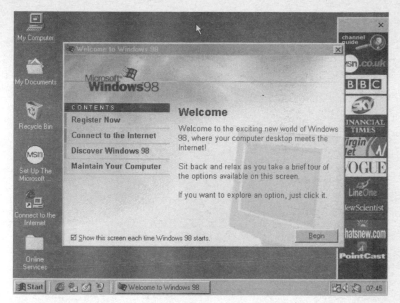

Fig.5.11 With installation complete some "fine tuning" may still be required

Advanced, and then monitor. This will bring up a screen like Figure 5.13 which shows the type of monitor that is installed, if it is not right left-click the Change button and select the correct one. If the picture is stable with the new settings but the size and position are completely wrong, there is probably no problem. It should be possible to position and size the picture correctly using the monitor's controls. Many graphics cards are supplied with utility software that helps to get the best possible display from the system, and it is worth trying any software of this type to see if it gives better results.

Windows 95/98 might have built-in support for all the hardware in your PC such as the sound and video cards, but this is unlikely. In order to get everything installed correctly you will probably require the installation discs provided with the various items of hardware used in the PC. These discs may be required during the installation of Windows 95/98, or they may have to be used after the basic installation has been completed. The instruction manuals provided with the hardware should explain the options available and provide precise installation instructions. These days even the motherboards seem to come complete with driver software

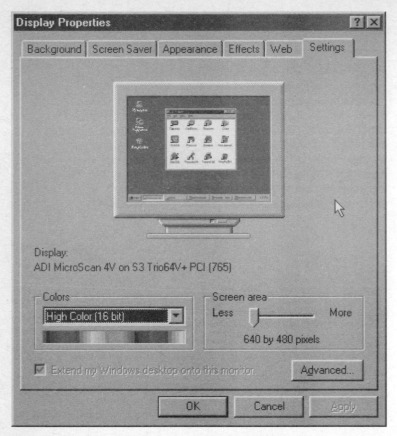

Fig.5.12 Using Control Panel to adjust the display settings

for things such as special chipset features and the hard disc interface. It is once again a matter of reading the instruction manual to determine which drivers have to be installed, and how to go about it. Get all the hardware properly installed before you install the applications software.

Once everything is supposedly installed correctly it is a good idea to go into the Control Panel program and double-click the System icon. Then select the Device Manager tab to bring up a window of the type shown in Figure 5.14. Look down the various entries to check for any problems, which will be indicated by a yellow question mark if Windows feels there might be a problem, or an exclamation mark if there is definitely a

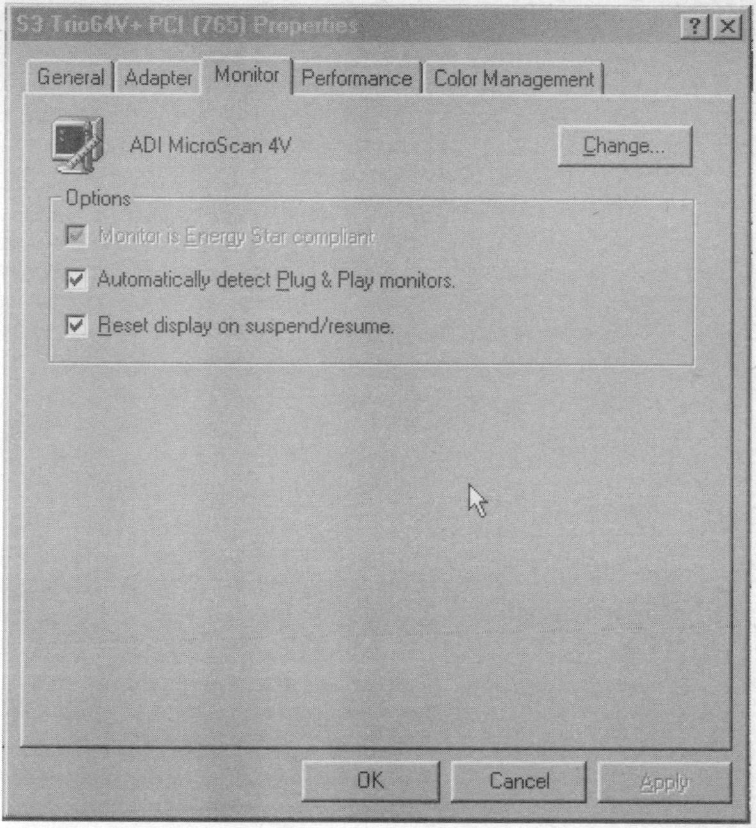

Fig.5.13 The Advanced settings enable the monitor type to be altered

problem. It does not show up very well in the grey scales of Figure 5.14, but there is an exclamation mark against the entry for primary IDE controller. The IDE interfaces are a common cause of problems. In some instances the cause of the trouble is Windows using a driver that is not quite right for the hard drive. Things may actually seem to work quite well, but there is a definite risk of problems occurring "somewhere down the line". The solution is to double-click on the entry in Device Manager, select Update Driver, and then get a list of all the available drivers (Figure 5.15). It is then a matter of trying likely drivers to sort out the problem. The standard IDE controller is a safe option, but is unlikely to give the ultimate in performance.

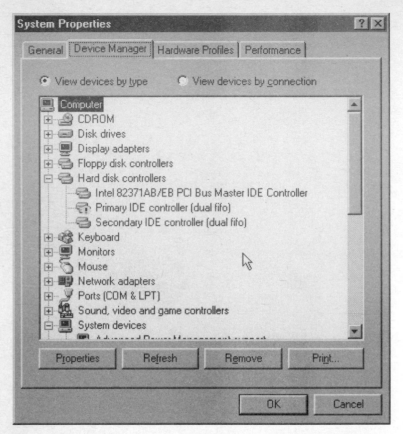

Fig.5.14 Checking for hardware problems using device manager

Assuming you are using a modern hard disc and motherboard, any problems with the hard disc controller will probably be due to a lack of the proper drivers. The motherboard should be supplied with a floppy disc or CD-ROM containing various drivers and other software. When using Windows 95 or 98 it is essential to read the relevant section of the motherboard's instruction manual, and to install the appropriate drivers. Windows may recognise the chipset in use and load the necessary drivers during the installation process, but in most cases some additional work will be needed in order to get the motherboard working at optimum efficiency.

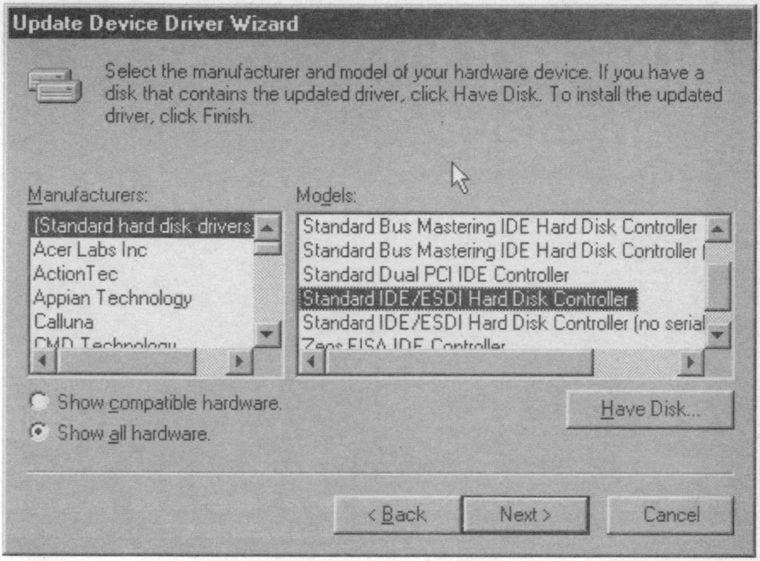

Fig.5.15 Getting a list of alternative drivers

If a problem is reported with the advanced power management control, this is most likely to be due to this facility being switched off in the BIOS. If you wish to use advanced power management you must obviously go into the BIOS Setup program and enable this feature. If not, simply leave things as they are. With most versions of Windows 95 there will be a problem reported with the USB ports. This is due to a lack of fully working USB support in these versions of Windows 95. If you do not require the USB ports it might be possible to disable them using the BIOS Setup program. It does not matter if this is not possible, since there should be no problems with these ports provided you do not try to use them. If you do require the USB ports the best option is to upgrade to Windows 98. The dreaded yellow exclamation marks in Device Manager should then disappear, and the ports should be fully operational.

Windows NT4

Windows NT4, and presumably Windows 2000 when it is finally released, can be installed from the bootable CD-ROM. To do this the CD-ROM must be set as a boot device using the BIOS Setup program, as described previously. With the Windows NT4 disc in the drive at switch-on the

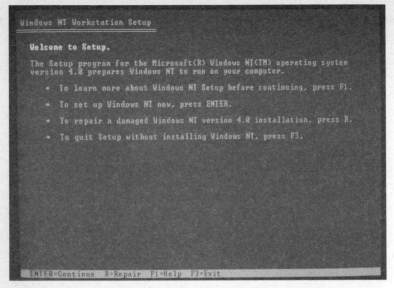

Fig.5.16 The initial screen of the Windows NT4 Setup program

computer should boot straight into an initial checking routine followed by the Setup program. This starts with a screen listing various options (Figure 5.16), but simple press the Enter key to proceed with installation. There is no need to bother with disc partitioning and formatting because the Setup program should detect the hard disc (Figure 5.17) and will give the option of preparing it for installation of the operating system (Figure 5.18). Note that Windows NT4 does not use FAT32, and a disc formatted using this system (and most others) is unusable in that form. The Setup program enables you to remove any partitions that are not suitably formatted, and the Setup program then prepares the disc for Windows NT4 to be installed.

Installing Windows NT4 is just the usual questions and answer style set up routine, with the inevitable reboots along the way. Like Windows 98, you have four installation options, and the "Typical" option is generally the best starting point. Unlike Windows 98, the use of a password is not optional, and you must supply one during installation. This will be needed each time the system is booted (Figure 5.19). You will have the option of connecting the PC to a network, but for a standalone PC the "Do not connect to a network at this time" option should be selected.

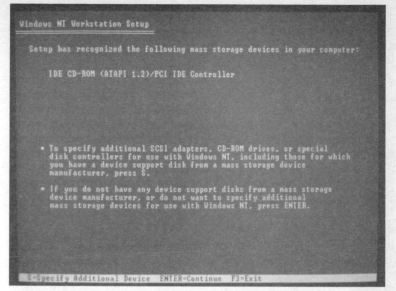

Fig.5.17 The Setup program should detect the hard disc

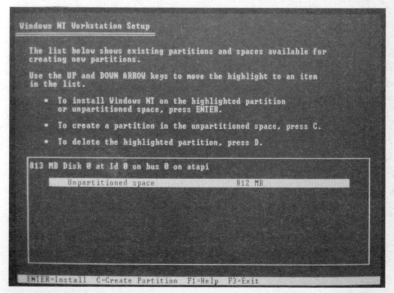

Fig.5.18 The Setup program can prepare the hard disc for installation

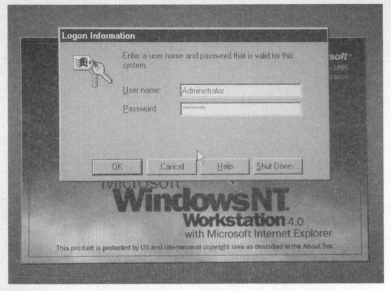

Fig.5.19 Use of a password is not optional with Windows NT4

Installing Windows NT4 is generally easier than installing Windows 95 or 98, but bear in mind that when the installation process is over, the PC is equipped with only a fairly basic but working version of the operating system (Figure 5.20). The display will probably be a simple VGA type unless your display card was detected and properly recognised during installation. If this happens the required resolution, colour depth, and scan frequency are set during installation. With Windows 98 there is no need to worry about scan frequencies, because the operating system knows the limits of the monitor and will keep within them. With Windows NT you are given several options, and you have to select the best one. In general this is the highest scan frequency that the monitor can handle. Its instruction manual should give its maximum scan rate for the standard screen resolutions. If you should set an excessive scan rate the display will fail the test routine that is used prior to finally selecting the required screen mode. Therefore, you can simply use the highest scan rate that works.

Even if the video card is fully operational, there will be little or no support for soundcards, etc. Consequently, some additional installation is required in order to get all the hardware fully operational. Unless you

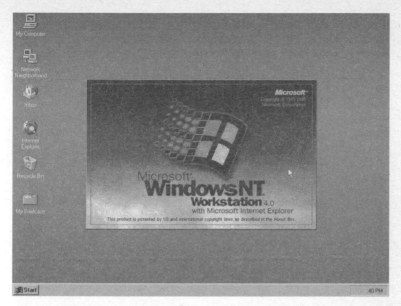

Fig.5.20 Windows NT4 installed, but some hardware drivers are still to be loaded

are using a recent version of Windows NT4 it will also be necessary to install the latest service pack in order to bring the installation up to date. At the time of writing this piece service pack five is the latest version.

Linux

Linux is available in various distributions and there have been numerous versions of each distribution. Consequently the exact method of installing this operating system varies somewhat from one version and distribution to another. Looking at things in broad terms there are currently two basic methods of installing Linux. Both of these involve installation direct from the Linux CD-ROM. With one method the CD-ROM is a bootable type, and to get installation underway it is just a matter of putting the CD-ROM in the drive and resetting the computer. If the CD-ROM drive has not been set as one of the boot drives, this must be done now. On exiting the BIOS Setup program the computer should boot from the Linux CD-ROM, and with most of the recent distributions of Linux the installation process is largely automatic.

If the distribution CD-ROM is not a bootable type it is usually possible to enter the installation program by booting into MS/DOS first. The easiest way to do this is to boot the computer using Windows 98 start-up disc, opting for CD-ROM support when prompted. Otherwise a MS/DOS boot disc must be used, and CD-ROM support must be added to this using the software supplied with the drive. There should be a text file on the CD-ROM that explains how to run the installation program. This should entail nothing more than going into the appropriate directory of the disc and running a program called something like "autoboot". The computer then exits MS/DOS and goes into a sort of mini-Linux operating system. The installation process then proceeds normally from there.

Linux partitions

With some distributions there is no need for the user to get embroiled with the Linux version of FDISK, but with others it is still necessary to partition the hard disc yourself. This may also be necessary if the installation program encounters a problem with the hard disc. Note that you should not use the MS/DOS FDISK program to partition the hard disc. Things should be much easier if you go into the Linux installation program with the hard disc totally blank. If you are going to use a dual boot system the best way of handling things is to create the partition or partitions for the other operating system, and then install that system onto the disc. Linux is then installed on the remaining disc space, which is partitioned and formatted during the installation process. The Linux boot manager ("LILO") can also be installed during the installation process.

Linux normally operates with a minimum of two disc partitions. One of these is used as a swap disc, which is simply some hard disc space that is set aside for the operating system to use as temporary storage space. This is typically equal to the amount of RAM in the PC, but there may be a limit of 100 megabytes on the size of this partition. The other partition is the main one where Linux is actually installed. Further partitions can be created if desired, but there is often no advantage in doing so.

Using FDISK

The Linux FDISK program is probably slightly trickier to use than the MS/DOS equivalent. Like its MS/DOS counterpart it uses a simple command line interface, where you issue commands by typing in the appropriate letter and then pressing the Return key. Any numeric data required by the program is also typed in at the command line. This is a list of the commands available when using FDISK:

Letter Command

a   Toggle a bootable flag on current partition

d   Delete current partition

l   List all partitions

m   Main menu

n   Create a new partition

p   Print a list of partitions with partition details

q   Quit without saving changes

r   Replace the system ID of the current partition

u   Modify the display/entry units (cylinders or sectors)

v   Verify

w   Save changes and exit

For the sake of this example we will assume that the PC will have Linux as the only operating system and that it has a hard disc capacity of 1000MB. With (say) 32MB of memory you will require a swap disc of at least 32MB, but might decide that a slightly larger capacity of 50MB would be better. This represents about five percent of the total disc space, which means that 95 percent is to be used for the main Linux installation. Create the main partition first, and pressing the "N" key (followed by the Return key of course). The computer responds with:

Command action

       e   Extended

       p   Primary partition (1-4)

You are being asked to select the partition type, and it is a primary partition that is required. Press the "P" key followed by Return. The computer responds with:

Partition number (1 - 4)

The partition being created is the first one on the hard disc, so type "1" followed by Return. You will then be asked to specify the numbers for the start and finish cylinders for the new partition, and the program will display the range of available numbers. As the hard disc is not being used with any other operating systems the first available cylinder should be number one. The highest number available depends on the size and characteristics of the disc, but for this example we will assume that there are 800 cylinders available. We wish to use the first 95 percent of the available cylinders, which works out at cylinders from 1 to 760. As an alternative to specifying the last cylinder you can enter the size of the partition in megabytes or kilobytes. For instance, typing "+950M" followed by Return would set the partition at 950MB. This second method is perhaps easier than specifying the final cylinder number, but you need to be careful, as there is something less than complete agreement about what constitutes a megabyte. It is easy to end up with an amount of space for the swap disc that is somewhat larger or smaller than you intended.

Swap partition

Next the partition for the swap disc must be created, and this is basically just a matter or repeating the steps above. This is the second partition on the disc, so give "2" as the partition number. The program should indicate the first and last cylinder numbers for the unused disc space. As we wish to use all this space for the swap disc, these numbers are used when setting the size of this partition. In our example installation the start and finish numbers will be 761 and 800. This creates the partition for the swap disc, but at present it is a standard Linux partition. It must be changed to a swap partition before it can be used for the swap disc. To do this press "T" followed by Return, and then "2" followed by a further Return to select the correct partition. The computer will respond with:

Hex code (type L to list codes):

If you type "L" followed by return you will be greeted with quite a large list of available partition types. At present the partition is type 83 (native Linux), and it must be changed to type 82 (Linux swap). To do this simply type "82" followed by Return. It is as well to check at this stage to see if everything has been set up correctly. Type "P" and then Return to bring up the partition table. In our example this would bring up something like:

Device	Boot	Start	End	Blocks	Id	System
/tmp/hda1		1	760	781234	83	Linux native
/tmp/hda2		761	800	39062	82	Linux swap

The entries under "Device" are the equivalents of MS/DOS and Windows drive letters. The important things to check are the sizes of the two partitions and that they are the correct types. If the partition types have been accidentally swapped over, they can be corrected using partition type command. If an error in the sizes has been made you will have to delete both partitions and start again. To delete a partition type "D" followed by Return, and then type the number of the partition to be deleted followed by a further Return.

FDISK will not automatically make the first primary partition bootable, and this is a common cause of problems when installing Linux as the sole operating system on a computer. If you omit this step the installation will proceed more or less normally, and everything will probably seem to be perfectly all right. At least, it will until you next use the computer. The computer then starts the boot-up process but simply hangs up or goes into a loop printing garbage down the screen. To make the first primary partition bootable press the "A" key followed by Return. The computer will respond with:

Partition number (1 - 4)

It is the first primary partition that must be made bootable, so press the "1" key followed by Return. To check that this has worked correctly print the partition table on the screen again. If all is well it should look something like this:

Device	Boot	Start	End	Blocks	Id	System
/tmp/hda1	*	1	760	781234	83	Linux native
/tmp/hda2		761	800	39062	82	Linux swap

To actually write the new partition information onto the hard disc press "W" followed by Return. You are then ready to continue with the installation process. If the Installation program asks you if there are any more changes to be made to the partitioning, answer no and continue with the installation. You may be asked to specify the mount point of the disc file system. Simply give this as "/".

Linux has built-in support for a massive range of hardware, but there tends to be a lag between new hardware appearing and support for it being provided by Linux. When building a PC for use with Linux it is a good idea to check carefully that the hardware you will be using, particularly the video card, is compatible with the version of Linux you wish to install.

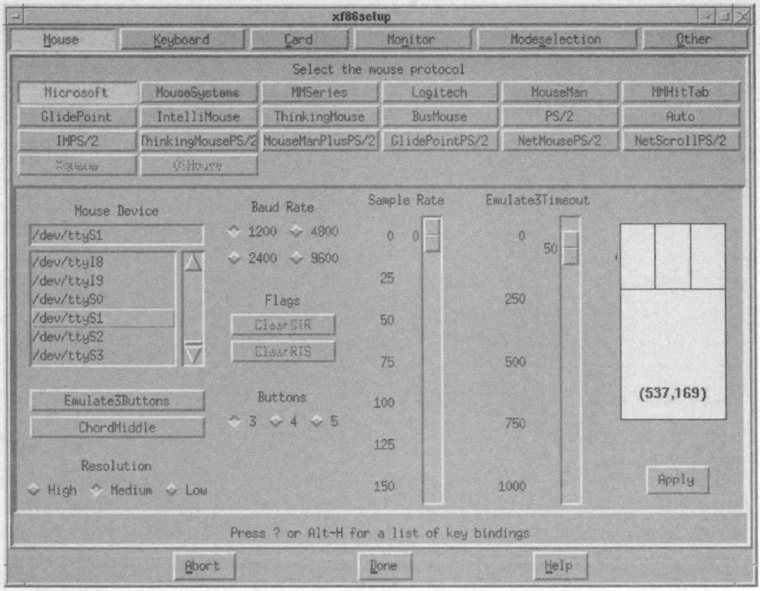

Fig.5.21 The mouse control screen of XF86Setup

KDE

If you only install a minimalist version of Linux you will have a text based operating system, like a sort of turbo-charged MS/DOS. In order to get the most from Linux you really need to install the X Windows system plus a program such as Gnome or KDE. The latter is probably the most popular graphical user interface (GUI) for Linux and is now included with most distributions. Modern distributions often require little input from the user in order to get X Windows configured correctly, but you may have to use the XF86Setup program to provide information about the keyboard, mouse, video card, etc. With its graphical user interface, as in the example screen of Figure 5.21, this program is reasonably easy to use, but it will probably be necessary to extract some technical information from the manuals for the video card and monitor. The mouse sometimes causes problems, because users of Logitech serial mice tend to select this option from the list of compatible mice. In fact modern Logitech serial mice are compatible with Microsoft serial mice, and either this option or the generic serial mouse should be selected.

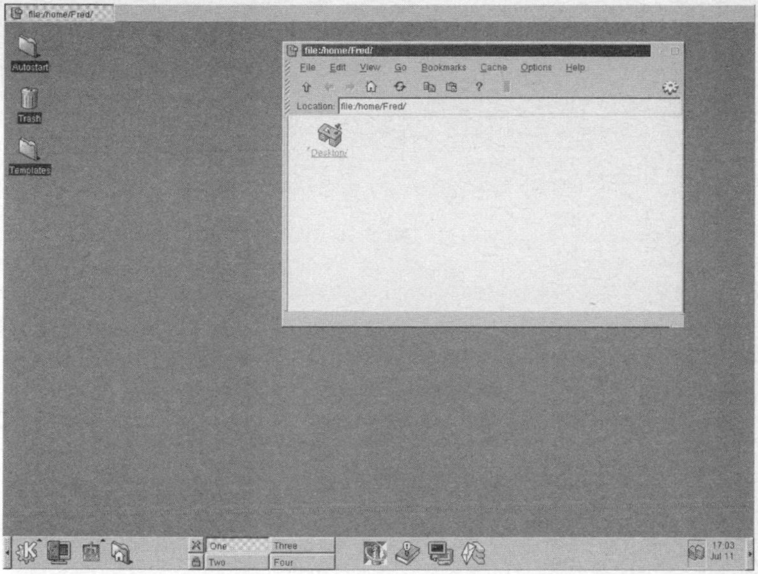

Fig.5.22 KDE provides a Windows style graphical user interface

Like Windows NT4, the use of passwords is mandatory with Linux. One password is needed for whoever supervises the computer, and additional passwords are required for each user. Most system administration is only possible if you sign in as the supervisor, or superuser to use the Linux terminology. Linux is a true multi-user operating system, and to each user it appears as though they have their own customised PC. They do not of course, but the password system enables Linux to use the appropriate configuration files for whoever is using the system. This gives what appears to be a PC customised to each user, and I suppose for all practical purposes they are. Once Linux and KDE are set up and running properly you should end up with a screen something like the one shown in Figure 5.22.

Points to remember

To place MS/DOS, MS/DOS and Windows 3.1, or Windows 95/98 onto the hard disc it must first be partitioned with the MS/DOS FDISK program. It must then be formatted with the MS/DOS FORMAT command. Choose support for large hard discs when it is offered (you are using an old version of FDISK if this option is not offered).

You must produce at least one partition on the disc, even if it will be used as a single drive. You produce one partition that utilizes all the disc's capacity. An extended partition can be created and used as one or more logical drives if required.

The easiest way to install Windows 95/98 is to boot from a Windows 98 Startup disc, selecting CD-ROM support from the initial menu. With the installation CD-ROM in the drive the Setup program can then be run. You will need to provide some information to the Setup program, and the installation discs supplied with the hardware may also be needed at some point, but installation is largely automatic.

Provided the BIOS has been set to make the CD-ROM drive one of the boot drives, it is possible to boot from the installation CD-ROMs of some operating systems. This is possible with Windows NT4 and most distributions of Linux, but not with Windows 95 or 98.

With Windows NT4 and most distributions of Linux you do not need to partition or format the hard disc prior to installation. Indeed, it is pointless to do so and may cause problems during installation. The disc will be partitioned and formatted during the installation process.

With some operating systems and hardware you may need to do further installation work once the Setup program has produced a basic installation. The instruction manuals provided with the hardware should give detailed installation instructions. You may also need to do some configuration, such as setting the required screen resolution and colour depth.

Troubleshooting

Prevention

Provided you proceed carefully, checking and double-checking everything as you go, and observing the basic anti-static handling precautions, you will be very unlucky indeed if the finished computer fails to start up correctly. However meticulous you are though, there is still an outside chance that things will not go perfectly, and if you take an "it will be all right on the night" approach to things it is likely that things will be far from all right when the new PC is switched on. This is definitely something where the old adage that "prevention is better than cure" applies. Most computer components are reasonably idiot-proof, and if an error should be made it is unlikely that any damage will occur. This possibility can not be totally ruled out though, and there is a small but real risk of mistakes proving to be quite costly. Check everything as you go along, and then carefully recheck the finished PC before switching it on.

Blank expression

A faulty PC may start to go through the initial start up routine and then fail at some stage, usually after the initial BIOS checks as the computer goes into the boot-up phase. Alternatively it may simply refuse to do anything, or sit there on the desk producing "beeping" noises with a blank screen. We will start by considering likely causes if the computer does very little, or even nothing at all.

If switching on the PC results in nothing happening at all, with no sign of cooling fans operating or front panel lights switching on, the obvious first step is to check that power is getting to the computer. Is the power lead plugged in properly at both the computer and the mains outlet, and is the mains supply switched on at the outlet? It is a silly mistake to forget to plug the computer into the mains supply or to switch on the supply, but it is easily done in your haste to try out the new PC. Also check that the fuse in the mains plug is present and correct.

A PC power supply is a fairly sophisticated piece of electronics that contains numerous protection circuits. The fact that it fails to operate even though it is receiving power does not necessarily mean that it is faulty. It could simply be that a protection circuit is detecting a problem somewhere and is shutting down the supply circuit. An overload on one of the supply lines could cause this, but is not a likely cause of the problem with a new PC. However, you can not totally rule out the possibility that the cause of the problem is a fault in one of the components that the supply is powering.

A more likely cause is that the leads carrying the output of the supply are not connected properly. With an AT supply it is possible to get the two supply connectors swapped at the motherboard. Fortunately, the supply should detect this problem and fail to switch on, ensuring that costly damage is avoided. With the power supply connected correctly the black leads should be grouped together in the middle (refer back to Figure 3.34 in chapter 3). If the black leads are at the ends of the row of leads the two connectors have been swapped over.

An ATX power supply only has one lead and connector that goes to the motherboard and this can only be connected the right way round. In theory this makes it impossible to get things wrong, but in practice this type of power connector can be difficult to get properly into place. In fact this applies to most types of power connector, and I suppose it is a byproduct of making the connectors fit very firmly together so that good connections are produced. It is worth removing and refitting the power connector to the motherboard to make quite sure that it is fully pressed down and into place. An ATX power supply is switched on and off via a simple pushbutton switch on the front of the case, and not by way of a conventional on/off switch in the mains supply. Check that the on/off switch is connected to the motherboard correctly.

If the mains supply seems to be getting through to the power supply unit all right, and the on/off switch and motherboard are connected to the power supply correctly, it is time to look further afield for the problem. It is unlikely that a faulty drive is causing an overload, but it is as well to check this by disconnecting the drive power leads. It is worth making the point that you should not disconnect and reconnect any leads with the computer switched on. Doing so with power or data leads could result in costly damage, with you creating more faults than you fix! If any changes to the cabling are required, switch off the computer, make the changes, and then switch on again. Ideally the drive data cables should also be disconnected when making this test. With no power supplied to the drives they could provide abnormal loading on the data cables and could conceivable cause damage to the motherboard, although the chances of this occurring are admittedly quite remote.

On the cards

If removing power from the drives does not effect a cure it is time to restore power to the drives and move on to the expansion cards. Switch off the computer, remove all the expansion cards, and then switch on again. In my experience the expansion cards are often the cause of problems, and removing them will often result in an otherwise "dead" PC bursting into life. If the cause of the problem is a faulty card, reinserting the cards one by one will soon reveal which card is at fault. When the computer ceases to start up again, the last card restored is the faulty one. Of course, the computer must be switched off before each card is installed. Adding or removing a card with the computer switched on does not guarantee that something will be damaged, but it nearly does.

Do not be surprised if having restored all the cards in the computer it still starts up properly. This will not be due to the faulty card having been miraculously cured, but is simply due to the fact that it was not originally installed correctly. If a card is not slotted into the motherboard correctly it can cause short circuits that will prevent the power supply from operating. The expansion card system used in PCs is a decided asset, which makes it easy to produce custom PCs that exactly suit given requirements. It also makes it easy to change the configuration of a PC to suit changing circumstances. The drawback of this system is that there are numerous contacts on the expansion card connectors, and the card and motherboard connectors must be accurately aligned if everything is to work properly. Some PCs fit together better than others, but it can sometimes be difficult to get the cards into place, and nothing seems to fit correctly. When this happens the usual cause is the motherboard being slightly out of position on the base panel of the case.

On the level

Do not simply wrestle with the expansion cards until they are eventually forced into place. Apart from the very real risk of damaging the cards and the motherboard, boards forced into place in this fashion are unlikely to stay in place very long. If expansion cards are proving troublesome it is usually possible to sort things out by slightly loosening the screws that hold the motherboard in place. Fit the expansion cards and then tighten the motherboard's mounting bolts again. You may occasionally

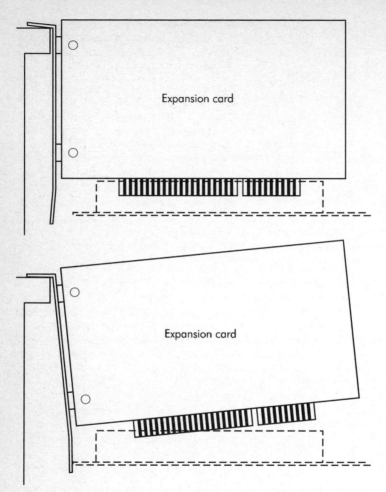

*Fig.6.1 A mounting bracket can cause problems if it is does not have
the correct right-angled bend*

find that an expansion card plugs into place perfectly well, but when its
retaining bolt is tightened it tends to lift up out of its expansion slot. In
most cases it is only the front end of the card that shifts out of position.
The usual cause of this is the metal mounting bracket on the card does
not having a proper 90-degree bend at the top where it bolts to the rear

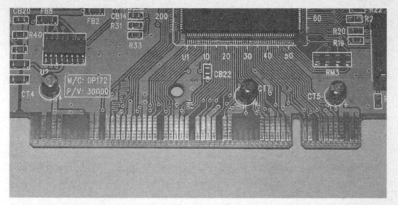

Fig.6.2 The gap between adjacent contacts on an expansion card is very small, making accurate alignment of the card and slot absolutely essential

of the case. This results in the card tending to lift out of the expansion slot at one end when the fixing bolt it tightened. This is shown in somewhat exaggerated form in Figure 6.1. In theory the bottom end of the bracket should slot into the case so that this can not happen, but in practice the card can often slip far enough out of alignment to give problems. The cure is to carefully bend the bracket to the correct angle with the aid of a small vice or some sturdy pliers.

Note that it only needs the card to lift slightly at one end or the other to totally "gum up" the computer. There are only minute gaps between the metal contacts on the connector of an expansion card (Figure 6.2). If the connector fits into the expansion slot at a slight angle this produces short-circuits along the rows of terminals. This in turn produces short-circuits on the supply lines, causing the power supply to shut down. With luck this should prevent any damage from occurring, but it is much better if you can spot a badly fitting card before you switch on the PC.

Another occasional cause of problems is a mounting bracket that is too high or too low on the expansion card. If it is mounted too low down on the card it will prevent the card from going down into the slot correctly. When this occurs it is usually possible to loosen the screws that fix the bracket to the card, pull the bracket into the correct position, and then retighten the screws.

Another problem with the expansion card system is that it only needs one bad connection to prevent the entire computer from working properly.

This is something that tends to be more of a problem after a computer has been in use for some time and the connectors start to corrode slightly. Nevertheless, even with new equipment it is possible that the metal terminals on one or other of the connectors could be slightly dirty or corroded, and that bad connections could cause problems. There are special cleaning fluids, etc., for use with connectors, but simply inserting and removing an expansion card a few times should do the trick.

The problem could be due to a faulty memory module short-circuiting the supply, and removing the module or modules from the motherboard might bring results. It could also be that the processor is faulty and is overloading the supply, but this is not very likely. It is not a good idea to power up the motherboard without a processor installed, so unless you have another processor that can be tried on the motherboard it is difficult to test for this.

Substitution

If none of this gets the power supply operating it is likely that either the motherboard or the power supply itself is faulty. Do not be tempted to open up the power supply unit and prod around inside to see if you can see what is wrong. A modern PC power supply is a complex piece of equipment that uses a lot of specialised components and quite advanced techniques. Many electronic engineers are not qualified to sort out this type of equipment and it is certainly well beyond the scope of an electronics handyman. Also, it is potentially lethal to dabble with any equipment that connects direct to the mains supply, and it is certainly not something that should be undertaken by anyone who is not properly qualified.

So how can you determine whether it is the supply or the motherboard that is at fault? Sorting out problematic PCs is much easier if you have some old parts that can be used as an aid to fault finding. This is one reason for me not recommending do-it-yourself PC building to people who have little or no previous experience with PCs. Most long standing PC users have a collection of old components that have been replaced by more up to date components. These days they often have one or two complete but ageing PCs. I would certainly recommend that you hold on to any PCs or PC components that are working and not totally obsolete, as these can often be useful when sorting out a troublesome PC. Items such as old PCI video cards and low capacity IDE hard disc drives (Figure 6.3) can be invaluable when trying to sort out a faulty PC.

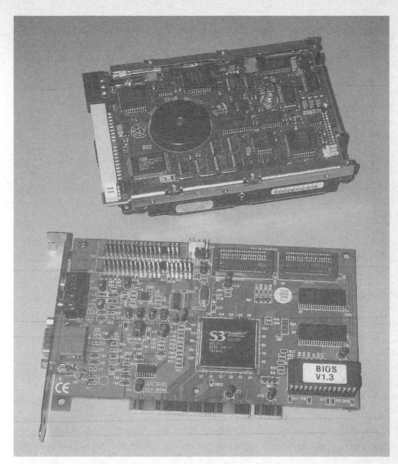

Fig.6.3 Keep old hard disc drives, video cards, etc. They can be invaluable when things go wrong

In this case an old motherboard could be temporarily installed in the case to see if the power supply can be persuaded to burst into action. Alternatively, the new motherboard could be installed in an old case to see if it functions correctly. In either example there could be problems if the new case and motherboard are of the ATX variety, and the old equipment has AT connectors. For some years now it has been standard practice for AT motherboards to be ATX compatible, so unless the "spare" motherboard is really old it should be compatible with a new case. If the new motherboard works in an old case, then clearly the new motherboard is not faulty. Presumably it is the new power supply that has the problem. If the old motherboard works properly in the new case, then the new power supply is functioning correctly and it is almost certainly the new motherboard that is faulty. This method of substituting a component that is known to work for one that is thought to be faulty is the basis for much PC faultfinding. Without specialised and expensive pieces of test equipment to check individual components it is the only practical method of determining which parts of a faulty PC work properly, and which do not.

Incidentally, if you return a component that is suspected of being faulty, it is unlikely to be tested on a special test bed or using some advanced piece of test equipment. It is much more likely that it will be installed in a working PC to see what happens. In other words, professional testers make great use of the substitution method, which is the quickest, easiest, and most reliable method of testing practically any computer component.

Partial failure

It is unusual for a faulty PC to simply "play dead" at switch-on, and the more usual problem is the computer starting up but reporting an error and failing to boot up. Sometimes it fails to boot because the error brings things to a halt before the boot-up phase is reached. In other cases the error message will include a phrase like "boot failure", which means that the BIOS has tried to boot the PC but has failed to find a valid operating system. We will consider pre-boot failures first.

If the computer seems to be starting up normally, but there is no video signal, the obvious first check is to see whether or not the video card is installed correctly. In my experience it is the video card that is most likely to give problems if there is a problem with physical alignment of the cards. Also check that the signal lead for the monitor is connected properly to the video card, and at the monitor if it is detachable at this end as well. If none of the monitor's indicator lights switch on it is likely that the problem is a complete lack of power to the monitor rather than an absence of video output from the computer. There is normally an indicator light switched on even if a modern monitor is receiving no video signal. Either another light switches on or the light changes colour when a video signal is received. If the monitor is completely "dead", it is not receiving power and the power lead and plug must be checked. If the monitor is powered via the power supply unit, try powering it directly

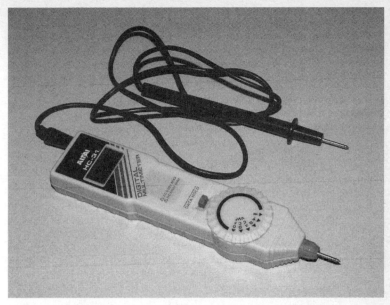

Fig.6.4 A digital test meter having a continuity tester function

from the mains supply. This will require a different power lead, but monitors can normally use a standard mains lead of the type used with most modern electrical and electronic gadgets. If necessary, borrow the computer's power lead and try using the monitor on its own. Obviously you will not get any response from the screen, but an indicator light should switch on if power is getting through to the monitor. If this results in it working, either the original power lead is faulty or the power supply unit is faulty and is not providing any power on the mains output socket.

Lead checking

When faultfinding on PCs you will soon need to check leads for broken wires. There are inexpensive test meters available that have a continuity tester setting that is ideal for this sort of thing. In addition to any visual indication, the unit normally produces a "beep" if a short-circuit is detected across the test prods. A miniature digital instrument (Figure 6.4) is well suited to this type of testing, but is somewhat over-specified. A basic analogue multimeter (Figure 6.5) is likely to be much cheaper

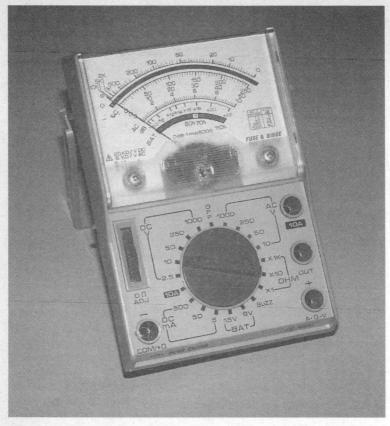

Fig.6.5 A cheap analogue multimeter is useful for checking leads

and will do the job well. In fact something much more basic is adequate for testing leads, and even an old torch bulb and battery style continuity checker (Figure 6.6) will do the job perfectly well. The test prods and leads can be the "real thing", but they need consist of nothing more than two pieces of single-strand insulated wire with a few millimetres of the insulation stripped away to produce the prods. This is admittedly a bit crude, but when testing computer leads it is often necessary to get the prods into tiny holes in the connectors. With the improvised prods there is no difficulty in doing so because they are so narrow, but with proper prods they are often too thick to fit into the connectors.

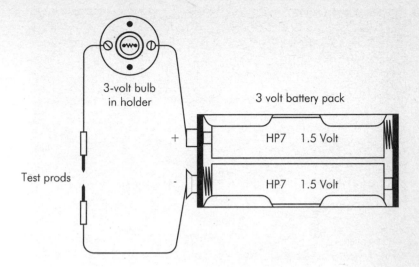

Fig.6.6 A simple continuity checker for testing leads

Testing cables is often rather awkward because you need four hands! One hand per test prod and another hand per connector. The easy way to tackle the problem is to fix both connectors to the workbench using clamps, or something like Bostik Blu-Tack or Plasticine will often do the job quite well (Figure 6.7). With heavier cables such as printer types it is better to clamp the connectors in place, because Blu-Tack and the like may not have sufficient sticking power to keep everything in place. With the connectors fixed to the bench and the metal terminals facing towards you it is easy to check for continuity because you then have both hands free to hold the test prods. Provided the workbench is well lit you can also see exactly what you are doing, which should help to avoid errors.

Incidentally, if you use a test meter for cable testing, on the face of it the meter is also suitable for checking the supply levels on the motherboard and other simple voltage checks. I would definitely advise against prodding around on the motherboard or an expansion card using a test meter. With the intricacy of modern boards it is quite tricky to do this, and there is a high risk of the test prods causing accidental short circuits. These could in turn ruin expensive items of hardware. The meter can be used to check for the correct voltages on a disc drive power cable, and for simple continuity tests on cables that have been totally removed from the PC, but it is advisable to go no further with it than that.

Fig.6.7 Fixing both connectors to the work table makes it much easier to test leads

Error messages

Returning to the subject of problems during the initial testing by the BIOS, it is possible for things to simply grind to a halt, but a more likely cause of the problem is that the BIOS has detected a problem and brought things to a halt. The screen may display a message along the lines "Press F1 to continue", but there is probably no point in trying to continue with the boot process if there is a major fault present in the system. The error message may be rather cryptic, giving nothing more than a number for the error. The computer may also do a certain number of "beeps" from the internal loudspeaker over and over again, which is another way of indicating the nature of the fault. Unfortunately, motherboard instruction manuals do not usually give any information about the exact meaning of the error messages, but this information might be available at the web site of the BIOS manufacturer. It is worthwhile looking in the manual to see if it gives any guidance. Some instruction manuals are much more comprehensive than others.

These days the error message usually gives some indication of what is causing the problem, with an error message along the lines "keyboard error or no keyboard present". With the BIOS telling you the cause of the problem you can obviously go straight to the component that has failed to work properly. It is then a matter of checking that the keyboard is connected correctly, the memory modules are seated correctly in their holders, or whatever.

Once again, the substitution method can be used to nail down the exact nature of the fault. If the BIOS reports something like a memory or keyboard problem and everything seems to be plugged in correctly, there is a tendency to jump to the conclusion that the keyboard or a memory module is faulty. This could well be the case, but it is also possible that the problem is due to a fault in the motherboard. If the keyboard is not functioning, try swapping over the keyboard with that of another PC. If the new PC fails to work with the replacement keyboard, but the other PC works perfectly well with the keyboard from the newly constructed PC, it is clearly the motherboard that is faulty. On the other hand, if the new PC works with the replacement keyboard and the other PC fails to work with the keyboard from the new PC, it is clearly the keyboard that is faulty.

Anomalies

Things in the computing world are not always as clear cut as they should be, and if you are very unlucky you may be faced with an anomaly. For example, in our keyboard substitution example you might find that on swapping the keyboards both computers work fine, but on swapping them back again the new PC fails to work again. I can not say that I have ever experienced this problem with keyboards, but I have certainly encountered one or two memory modules and expansion cards that are rather selective about the computers they will work in. I have also heard of others having similar problems with mice and CD-ROM drives.

It is difficult to explain this sort of thing, and there is probably more than one cause. In days gone by there were certainly problems with expansion slots and cards that were not engineered with adequate accuracy. Some combinations of motherboard and expansion card would just about fit together well enough to work while others would not. This sort of thing seems to be extremely rare these days, and the more likely cause of problems is some slight electrical incompatibility, or two components in the system refusing to peacefully coexist for some obscure reason. Some makes of hard disc drive do not get on well together for example, particularly when trying to use an old drive alongside a new one. Some CD-ROM drives and hard drives seem to suffer from a lack of compatibility.

If you are unlucky enough to find yourself saddled with one of these incompatibility problems you may be entitled to return the item that is causing the trouble. The difficulty is in determining which component is the cause of the problem, and it is understandable if suppliers are reluctant to take back items that work fine when they try them in their test PCs. If you persist with your complaint most suppliers will reluctantly do so, but you may prefer to be pragmatic about this sort of thing and rearrange the PCs slightly so that they all work, and the incompatibilities are avoided. It is probably not worthwhile spending large amounts of time trying to get incompatible components to function together. Bitter experience suggests that in most instances they will never do so.

Memory and processor

In some cases the BIOS will detect and report a memory problem, but if there is a total failure of the memory circuits or a problem with the processor the BIOS start-up routine may grind to a halt or never get started properly in the first place. When a memory fault is suspected, carefully check again the section of the motherboard's manual that deals with memory matters. Make sure that you are using an acceptable memory arrangement, and that the motherboard is not fitted with an unacceptable mixture of memory types. Although DIMMs can usually be used in multiples of one, SIMMs normally have to be used in pairs. With a single DIMM or one pair of SIMMs you might have to fit the modules in the correct bank of sockets for the memory to work correctly. The motherboard will probably not accept all SIMM and DIMM capacities. Are you using memory modules that are supported by the motherboard? Where the motherboard has provision for both DIMMs and SIMMs it will probably not be possible to use all the memory sockets. In some cases a mixture of DIMMs and SIMMs is not allowed at all, and in others the DIMM holders and one pair of SIMM sockets effectively occupy the same section of memory, and you can therefore only use one of the other. Modern motherboards are generally more accommodating than those of a few years ago, but when choosing the memory for a modern PC it is still essential to read the "small print" in the relevant section of the motherboard's manual.

A problem with the memory is most likely to be caused by one of the memory modules not fitting into its holder correctly. The quality of holders for memory modules is often quite poor even on some of the more up-market motherboards. This tends to make it quite difficult to fit the modules into the holders, and in some cases they can be difficult to

*Fig.6.8 A SIMM apparently fitted into its socket, but it is actually the
wrong way around*

remove as well. Look carefully at the modules and make quite sure that
they fit right down into the holders. When in place correctly the modules
should lock into position, so try giving the modules a gentle tug to see if
they pull free from the holders. If a module pulls away from its holder,
even at just one end, it is not fitted in the holder correctly. Although it
should not be possible to fit a SIMM the wrong way round, some SIMM
holders are so low in quality that this can actually be done. If this should
happen, on close inspection the module will clearly be seen to be off-
centre and (or) it will not fit into its holder correctly at one end (Figures
6.8 and 6.9).

DIMMs are less problematic than SIMMs, but check that the DIMMs are
fully pushed down into their sockets and locked in place. If a DIMM is
fully pushed down into its holder the locking arms on the holder should
fit into the cutouts at the ends of the module. One end of a properly
locked DIMM is shown in the close-up shot of Figure 6.10. With two
polarising keys, one of which is well off-centre, there is no excuse for
trying to fit a DIMM the wrong way around, and it should not even start
to fit into the holder. Whenever problems with the memory are suspected
it is a good idea to remove the memory modules and refit them. This
often seems to cure the problem.

*Fig.6.9 In this close-up view it is apparent that the SIMM is not
properly in the socket at one end*

The chance of a problem occurring with the microprocessor are very
low, because the processor will only fit onto the motherboard the right
way round, and very high quality ZIF sockets are used on even the
cheaper motherboards. If the processor fails to function properly the
most likely cause is the motherboard being configured incorrectly. If
the motherboard has some form of automatic processor detection facility,
check that the right processor is specified on the initial start-up screen.
If the wrong processor is identified it will be necessary to go into the
appropriate section of the BIOS Setup program and set the processor
parameters manually. Note that if you are using a processor that has a
clock frequency that is actually lower than its "equivalent" speed rating,
it may well be the true clock frequency that the BIOS will use on the
initial start-up screen. This depends on whether or not the BIOS
specifically supports the processor you are using. Obviously there is a
problem if the reported speed does not match up with the nominal or
actual clock frequency of the processor. If the motherboard is configured
via jumpers or DIP switches, check the motherboard's instruction manual
carefully again to ensure that you are using precisely the required
settings.

Fig.6.10 A close-up showing the locking arm of a holder within the notch of a DIMM

Discs

Discs and the BIOS were covered in chapter 4, and this topic will not be covered in detail again here. If you have not gone into the BIOS Setup program and set suitable drive settings it is unlikely that they will all function correctly. As pointed out previously, there can be problems with incompatibility between certain IDE devices. This mainly occurs when using an old hard disc drive and a new one, and it can also occur when using some hard drive and CD-ROM combinations. This seems to be an innate problem with the drives, but it can often be resolved by shifting one of the drives from one IDE interface to another. In most cases this means having the problem devices on separate IDE interfaces, but apparently in some cases it can be necessary to move them from separate interfaces to the same IDE channel.

Note that if you are using an Ultra DMA33 or Ultra DMA66 hard disc drive, special drivers will be needed in order to get maximum performance from these. The motherboard and (or) drive should be supplied with

Windows 95/98 drivers and full installation instructions. Remember also, that Ultra DMA66 hard drives require a cable specifically for this type of drive and not an ordinary IDE cable.

Floppy problems

The most common mistake with floppy disc drives is to get one of the connectors fitted the wrong way round. If you try to boot from the floppy drive it is inevitably unsuccessful, but it can also result in the data on the disc being corrupted. Having cleared the fault you try to boot from the disc, but this again proves to be unsuccessful. This gives the impression that the floppy disc drive is faulty or still installed incorrectly, but it is actually the corrupted disc that is causing the problem. It is advisable to have one or two spare boot discs handy so that you can try an alternative disc if the computer refuses to boot from the floppy disc for no apparent reason.

If there is a problem with a floppy connector fitted the wrong way round, or with the wrong ends of the cable connected to the drive and the motherboard, this should be immediately obvious. During the initial BIOS checks and the boot-up sequence the drive light of the floppy disc drive will usually switch on and off a few times, but with the cable connected wrongly the light usually stays on continuously. If the drive light comes on at switch-on and stays on, switch off and check the data cable.

Late problems

Problems do not always come to light when a PC is going through its initial testing. Everything might seem to be all right until the operating system has been installed, after which some of the hardware may fail to work properly. Having installed Windows 95 or 98 on a new PC it is always a good idea to go into the Windows Device Manager to check for any problems. To do

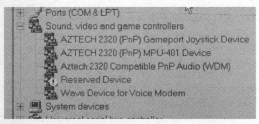

Fig.6.11 The exclamation mark indicates a problem with one of the soundcard drivers

this, operate the Start button and then select Settings, Control Panel, System, and operate the Device Manager tab. You can then look down the list of devices in search of the dreaded yellow exclamation marks that indicate a problem (Figure 6.11). Initially there will usually be a few problems reported by the Device Manager, and this is simply because some of the drivers for the motherboard's built-in hardware have not been installed. These days motherboards are invariably supplied with a disc and (or) CD-ROM with various driver programs that have to be installed before everything will operate to perfection. The motherboard's instruction manual should give full details of the drivers provided, and how to install them. With the particular configuration you are using you may not need all the drivers supplied, so read the manual carefully to determine which software must be installed.

The ports can often be switched on and off via the BIOS Setup program, so if there is a problem with a port it is as well to go into the BIOS and check that any absent port is actually turned on. If a port is active, but is not detected by the operating system or an error is reported, it is likely that the port hardware is faulty. Unfortunately, since the standard ports are integrated with the motherboard these days, this means that the motherboard is faulty and must be replaced. One possible exception is if you are having problems with the USB ports under Windows 95. Most versions of Windows 95 do not have proper USB support, and it Is advisable to upgrade to Windows 98 if you intend to use the USB ports.

Right leads

When you have been building PCs for some time you inevitably end up with a lot of leads and other odds and ends. When building a PC based on an AT motherboard it is tempting to simply grab the first serial or parallel port lead and blanking plate that comes to hand. This is not really a good idea though, since leads that look much the same may actually be wired up very differently. The serial and parallel port leads supplied with motherboards are not all the same, and you could certainly end up with a non-operating port by using the lead from one motherboard with a different motherboard.

When dealing with apparently faulty serial and parallel ports on AT motherboards it can be helpful to use a continuity check to determine whether or not the port is connected properly to the motherboard. However, a torch bulb continuity tester of the type described earlier is not suitable for this type of testing. The test current used is too high, and could damage the port hardware. Only use a proper test meter that

connectors one row of pins out of alignment. Fortunately, these cut-down connectors are now relatively rare, but due care needs to be taken if you should encounter a motherboard that uses them.

Minor problems

Most problems with a newly constructed PC are actually quite minor. Probably the most common of these is one of the front panel lights failing to operate. As pointed out in chapter three, these lights are light emitting diodes (LEDs) and not miniature light bulbs. Consequently they will only operate properly if they are fed with a supply of the correct polarity. If a light fails to operate, try reversing the connector to see if that cures the problem. If the integral loudspeaker or any of the LEDs and switches that connect to the motherboard fail to work, carefully check the connections to the connector block on the motherboard. Getting these items plugged into the motherboard tends to be a bit fiddly, and it is often difficult to see what you are doing. Unless you have small fingers it will probably be easier using a pair of long-nose pliers or tweezers to manoeuvre the connectors into position.

Fig.6.15 The power LED connector is out of position

Incidentally, these tools are also useful for setting jumpers on the motherboard. If necessary shine a torch on the connector block so that you can see exactly what connects to where. It is easy to get a plug shifted along the block by one set of pins so that one pin is unconnected, or it connects to the wrong pins. In the example of Figure 6.15 the power LED connector is shifted one row of pins to the left. A close visual inspection should soon reveal any problem of this type.

Fig.6.16 A completed and working budget Socket 7 PC. The CD-ROM drive on this one was reluctant to operate due to its loose fitting data cable, but a change to a different cable cured the problem

Finally

Obscure problems can occur with a new PC, but they are relatively rare with modern PCs. In the vast majority of cases the computer will boot-up properly and work well if you are careful to get everything connected properly. When a newly assembled PC fails to work properly it is hardly ever due to a faulty component, and is usually due to something very fundamental like a connector that has come adrift or is fitted the wrong way around. When something goes wrong we would all rather blame someone else, but if you check through a troublesome PC and fix any mistakes it will almost certainly work flawlessly when you try it out again.

Points to remember

Prevention is better than cure, so always give the finished PC at least a cursory check before switching on and testing it. Ideally you should check that all the cables are present and correct.

Again, prevention is better than cure, so do not be tempted to ignore anti-static handling precautions. It will be time consuming and costly to replace components that were unnecessarily "zapped" by a static charge.

Check for the obvious, such as a lead that has become disconnected at one end, or drive power cable you have forgotten to plug in. In the vast majority of cases where a newly constructed PC fails to work it is something as simple as this.

If the motherboard uses configuration jumpers or switches, check that it is configured properly for the processor you are using. The configuration charts in motherboard instruction manuals are sometimes a bit ambiguous, so check them with a "fine-tooth comb" to ensure you are interpreting them correctly.

Check that the expansion cards are all properly seated in their holders. It only needs one of the cards to be slightly out of position to render the PC completely inoperative.

Try reducing the computer to one that is as basic as possible. Disconnect the hard disc drive, CD-ROM drive, and any non-essential expansion cards so that the PC is just a basic single floppy machine. If this works, reinstate the drives, etc., one by one until the PC fails to work. The last device added is then the one that is causing the problem.

Check that the memory modules are fitted into their holders properly. DIMMs are reasonably foolproof, but SIMMs can and do give problems unless you are very careful when fitting them.

Never connect or disconnect anything while the PC is switched on. Altering the cabling while a PC is switched on could easily cause costly damage.

Definitely do not add or remove an expansion card or a memory module while the PC is switched on. This virtually guarantees that something will be damaged.

If an expansion card is suspected of being faulty, the easiest way to test it is to use it in another PC. Alternatively, try another expansion card in the PC that is giving problems.

Keep old video cards, hard disc drives, etc. They are useful for substituting in a faulty PC to help track down the duff component. It is obviously not worthwhile keeping anything that is totally obsolete and not usable in a modern PC, but anything else is potentially useful.

Faulty components in new PCs are actually quite rare. If you get everything put together properly it is highly unlikely that your new PC will fail to work.

Never be tempted to open up the power supply unit. It is not the sort of thing that can be sorted by the average handyman, or even those with some knowledge of electronics. The power supply connects to the mains supply and is potentially lethal. If a power supply unit is found to be faulty, either the power supply or the complete case and power supply should be replaced.

Appendix 1

Useful Web addresses 1

http://www.abit.com.tw	Abit
http://www.aopenusa.com	Aopen
http://www.asus.com.tw	Asustec
http://www.chaintech.com.tw	Chaintech
http://www.ecsusa.com	Elitegroup
http://www.Gigabyte.com	Gigabyte
http://www.gbt_tech.co.uk	Gigabyte (UK)
http://www.iwillusa.com	Iwill
http://www.jetway.com.tw	Jetway
http://www.pcchips.com	PC Chips
http://www.qdigrp.com	QDI
http://www.qdi.nl/english	QDI (UK)
http://www.mycomp-tmc.com	TMC
http://www.supermicro.com	Supermicro
http://www.soyo.com.tw	Soyo
http://www.tyan.com	Tyan
http://www.tekram.com	Tekram

This is a list of the web addresses for a range of motherboard manufacturers. The name of the company concerned is usually apparent from the address, but the manufacturer's name is given anyway. Where two addresses are given for one manufacturer, one is the main site and the other is a UK specific site. For prospective PC builders it is well worthwhile visiting the web sites of some motherboard manufacturers, where you will find detailed information on their products. In many cases the instruction manuals for the boards are also available, and a great deal can be learned by looking through some of these.

Appendix 2

Useful Web addresses 2

http://www.3com.co.uk	3Com (modems)
http://www.atitech.com	ATI (graphics cards)
http://www.cle.creaf.com	Creative Labs (sound, graphics)
http://www.diamondmm.com	Diamond (sound, graphics)
http://www.fujitsu.computers.com	Fujitsu (hard discs)
http://www.hercules.com	Hercules (graphics)
http://www.uk.ibm.com	IBM (hard discs)
http://www.matrox.com	Matrox (graphics)
http://www.quantum.com	Quantum (hard discs)
http://www.seagate.com	Seagate (hard discs)
http://www.stb.com	STB (sound, graphics)
http://www.wdc.com	Western Digital (hard discs)
http://www.yamaha.co.uk	Yamaha (soundcards)

This is a list of the web sites for some of the main manufacturers of soundcards, graphics cards, hard discs, etc. These sites contain a great deal of useful information in addition to detailed specifications for the products on offer. Instuction manuals for some of the hard disc drives can be downloaded, and a great deal can be learnt from these.

Index

Index

Index